most loved recipe collection most loved recipe collection

August 1, 2009
from Peter Jr.

most loved

Summertime
DESSERTS

Pictured on front cover:
Pavlova, page 36

Pictured on back cover:
Sundae Dessert, page 98

Most Loved Summertime Desserts
Copyright © Company's Coming Publishing Limited

First Printing April 2008

Library and Archives Canada Cataloguing in Publication
Paré, Jean, date-
Most loved summertime desserts / Jean Paré.
(Most loved recipe collection)
Includes index.
ISBN 978-1-897069-52-3
1. Desserts. I. Title. II. Series: Paré, Jean, date- . Most loved recipe collection.
TX773.P359115 2008   641.8'6   C2007-904695-9

Published by
Company's Coming Publishing Limited
2311 – 96 Street
Edmonton, Alberta, Canada T6N 1G3
Tel: 780-450-6223   Fax: 780-450-1857
www.companyscoming.com

Company's Coming is a registered trademark owned by
Company's Coming Publishing Limited

We acknowledge the financial support of the Government of Canada through the Book Publishing Industry Development Program (BPIDP) for our publishing activities.

Printed in China

We gratefully acknowledge the following suppliers for their generous support of our Test and Photography Kitchens:

Broil King Barbecues
Corelle®
Hamilton Beach® Canada
Lagostina®
Proctor Silex® Canada
Tupperware®

Our special thanks to the following businesses for providing props for photography:

Casa Bugatti
Cherison Enterprises Inc.
Chintz & Company
Danesco Inc.
Home Outfitters
Mikasa Home Store
Pfaltzgraff Canada
Pier 1 Imports
Stokes
The Bay
Winners Stores

Pictured from left: Fruit Pizza, page 6; Chilled Chocolate Dessert, page 68; Mango Macadamia Sandwich, page 94; Peachsicle Slice, page 95; Strawberry Freeze, page 102

table of contents

the Company's Coming story

"never share a recipe you wouldn't use yourself"

Jean Paré (pronounced "jeen PAIR-ee") grew up understanding that the combination of family, friends and home cooking is the best recipe for a good life. From her mother, she learned to appreciate good cooking, while her father praised even her earliest attempts in the kitchen. When Jean left home, she took with her a love of cooking, many family recipes and an intriguing desire to read cookbooks as if they were novels!

In 1963, when her four children had all reached school age, Jean volunteered to cater the 50th Anniversary of the Vermilion School of Agriculture, now Lakeland College, in Alberta, Canada. Working out of her home, Jean prepared a dinner for more than 1,000 people, which launched a flourishing catering operation that continued for over 18 years. During that time, she had countless opportunities to test new ideas with immediate feedback—resulting in empty plates and contented customers! Whether preparing cocktail sandwiches for a house party or serving a hot meal for 1,500 people, Jean Paré earned a reputation for good food, courteous service and reasonable prices.

As requests for her recipes mounted, Jean was often asked the question, "Why don't you write a cookbook?" Jean responded by teaming up with her son, Grant Lovig, in the fall of 1980 to form Company's Coming Publishing Limited. The publication of *150 Delicious Squares* on April 14, 1981 marked the debut of what would soon become one of the world's most popular cookbook series.

The company has grown since those early days when Jean worked from a spare bedroom in her home. Today, she continues to write recipes while working closely with the staff of the Recipe Factory, as the Company's Coming test kitchen is affectionately known. There she fills the role of mentor, assisting with the development of recipes people most want to use for everyday cooking and easy entertaining. Every Company's Coming recipe is *kitchen-tested* before it's approved for publication.

Jean's daughter, Gail Lovig, is responsible for marketing and distribution, leading a team that includes sales personnel located in major cities across Canada. In addition, Company's Coming cookbooks are published and distributed under licence in the United States, Australia and other world markets. Bestsellers many times over in English, Company's Coming cookbooks have also been published in French and Spanish.

Familiar and trusted in home kitchens around the world, Company's Coming cookbooks are offered in a variety of formats. Highly regarded as kitchen workbooks, the softcover Original Series, with its lay-flat plastic comb binding, is still a favourite among readers.

Jean Paré's approach to cooking has always called for *quick and easy recipes* using *everyday ingredients.* That view has served her well. The recipient of many awards, including the Queen Elizabeth Golden Jubilee medal, Jean was appointed a Member of the Order of Canada, her country's highest lifetime achievement honour.

Jean continues to gain new supporters by adhering to what she calls The Golden Rule of Cooking: *"Never share a recipe you wouldn't use yourself."* It's an approach that works—*millions of times over!*

foreword

I love when spring turns to summer, the birds sing and all the gardens fill with flowers. And as the season changes, so do people. We break free from our winter cocoons of parkas and sweaters. We stop craving warm, filling foods, and turn to the cool, the light and the refreshing. That's where *Most Loved Summertime Desserts* comes in. While winter desserts are all about seeking comfort from the cold weather outside, summer desserts are a celebration of everything that is balmy, fresh, sunny and light.

Embrace all of Summer's Bounty with desserts from our fresh fruit chapter. Succulent Saskatoon Pie is a true Canadian classic, while balsamic-glazed Grilled Peaches will add an elegant touch to any barbecued meal.

If you like to spend time outdoors on summer evenings, you'll love our Light As Air section—crisp, airy Pavlova or a slice of fluffy Orange Chiffon Cake will satisfy without filling you up too much for gardening, bike riding or a sunset walk in the park.

How about the times when you want to savour the lazy, hazy days of summer and just enjoy Chilling Out? The desserts in the chilled section are perfect for making in the morning and storing in the fridge to ensure you'll have something cool and sweet at hand when you need it. Creamy Chocolate Raspberry Cheesecake or tangy Strawberry Margarita Pie are sure to provide a decadent, yet relaxed, finish to any meal.

And if you cherish your childhood memories of buying treats from the neighbourhood ice cream truck, you can rediscover familiar favourites like Banana Splits and Frozen Fudge Bars with our Beating the Heat frozen section. Or try the elegant Ginger Sorbet With Grilled Mangoes for a more grown-up treat.

Light and airy, refreshing and cool, these desserts are so delicious you'll be tempted to enjoy them all year long. Summer is short, so make the most of it with *Most Loved Summertime Desserts*.

Jean Paré

nutrition information

Each recipe is analyzed using the most current version of the Canadian Nutrient File from Health Canada, which is based on the United States Department of Agriculture (USDA) Nutrient Database.

- If more than one ingredient is listed (such as "butter or hard margarine"), or if a range is given (1 – 2 tsp., 5 – 10 mL), only the first ingredient or first amount is analyzed.

- For meat, poultry and fish, the serving size per person is based on the recommended 4 oz. (113 g) uncooked weight (without bone), which is 2 – 3 oz. (57 – 85 g) cooked weight (without bone)—approximately the size of a deck of playing cards.

- Milk used is 1% M.F. (milk fat), unless otherwise stated.

- Cooking oil used is canola oil, unless otherwise stated.

- Ingredients indicating "sprinkle," "optional," or "for garnish" are not included in the nutrition information.

- The fat in recipes and combination foods can vary greatly depending on the sources and types of fats used in each specific ingredient. For these reasons, the amount of saturated, monounsaturated and polyunsaturated fats may not add up to the total fat content.

Vera C. Mazurak, Ph.D.
Nutritionist

Pictured on page 3 and at right.

Fruit and pizza crust do indeed go together, and the proof is in this delicious and spectacular-looking dessert.

about kiwifruits

It's what's on the inside that counts! The first person to look at a kiwifruit probably never guessed what a deliciously tangy and vividly coloured interior hid beneath that strangely hairy skin. Named after the kiwi bird—a similarly shaped brown and hairy bird native to New Zealand— kiwifruits are available in both green and golden varieties. When selecting a kiwi, keep in mind that the firmer the fruit, the more tart it will be, and the softer the fruit, the sweeter it will be. Kiwis will continue to ripen if kept at room temperature, but will keep in the fridge for about three weeks.

Fruit Pizza

SUGARY PIZZA CRUST

All-purpose flour	1 1/4 cups	300 mL
Butter (or hard margarine), softened	2/3 cup	150 mL
Granulated sugar	1/2 cup	125 mL

TOPPING

Block of light cream cheese, softened	8 oz.	250 g
Icing (confectioner's) sugar	1/3 cup	75 mL
Vanilla extract	1 tsp.	5 mL
Can of mandarin orange segments, drained	10 oz.	284 mL
Fresh blueberries	1/2 cup	125 mL
Fresh strawberries, halved lengthwise	24	24
Kiwifruit, sliced	8	8

GLAZE

Apricot (or peach) jam	1/4 cup	60 mL
Hot water	1 tbsp.	15 mL

Sugary Pizza Crust: Mix all 3 ingredients in medium bowl until mixture forms a ball. Press firmly in ungreased 12 inch (30 cm) pizza pan, forming rim around edge. Bake on centre rack in 350°F (175°C) oven for about 12 minutes until golden. Cool.

Topping: Beat first 3 ingredients in small bowl until smooth. Spread evenly over crust.

Arrange next 4 ingredients in attractive pattern over cream cheese mixture.

Glaze: Combine jam and hot water in small cup. Brush over fruit. Chill. Cuts into 12 wedges.

1 wedge: 165 Calories; 13.3 g Total Fat (2.7 g Mono, 0.6 g Poly, 8.5 g Sat); 36 mg Cholesterol; 39 g Carbohydrate; 3 g Fibre; 4 g Protein; 165 mg Sodium

Pictured on page 3 and at right.

Strawberry Rhubarb Pie

Pastry for 2 crust 9 inch (22 cm) pie

Large egg	1	1
Granulated sugar	1 cup	250 mL
All-purpose flour	3 tbsp.	50 mL
Fresh rhubarb, chopped	3 cups	750 mL
Sliced fresh strawberries	1 cup	250 mL
Granulated sugar	1/2 tsp.	2 mL

Divide pastry into 2 portions, making 1 portion slightly larger than the other. Shape each portion into slightly flattened disc. Roll out larger portion on lightly floured surface to about 1/8 inch (3 mm) thickness. Line 9 inch (22 cm) pie plate.

Beat egg in large bowl. Add first amount of sugar and flour. Mix well. Add rhubarb and strawberries. Stir. Spread evenly in shell. Roll out smaller pastry portion on lightly floured surface to about 1/8 inch (3 mm) thickness. Dampen edge of pastry shell with water. Cover with pastry. Trim and crimp decorative edge to seal. Cut several small vents in top to allow steam to escape.

Sprinkle with second amount of sugar. Bake on bottom rack in 350°F (175°C) oven for about 45 minutes until browned and fruit is tender. Cuts into 8 wedges.

1 wedge: 369 Calories; 14.8 g Total Fat (0.3 g Mono, 0.2 g Poly, 6.2 g Sat); 33 mg Cholesterol; 56 g Carbohydrate; 1 g Fibre; 4 g Protein; 210 mg Sodium

Pictured on page 11.

Fresh Saskatoon Pie

Pastry for 2 crust 9 inch (22 cm) pie

Granulated sugar	1 cup	250 mL
All-purpose flour	1/4 cup	60 mL
Ground cinnamon	1/4 tsp.	1 mL
Salt	1/4 tsp.	1 mL
Fresh saskatoons	4 cups	1 L
Lemon juice	1 1/2 tbsp.	25 mL
Granulated sugar	1/2 tsp.	2 mL

(continued on next page)

Divide pastry into 2 portions, making 1 portion slightly larger than the other. Shape each portion into slightly flattened disc. Roll out larger portion on lightly floured surface to about 1/8 inch (3 mm) thickness. Line 9 inch (22 cm) pie plate.

Combine next 4 ingredients in large bowl. Add saskatoons. Stir. Spread evenly in shell.

Drizzle lemon juice over top. Roll out smaller pastry portion on lightly floured surface to about 1/8 inch (3 mm) thickness. Dampen edge of pastry shell with water. Cover with pastry. Trim and crimp decorative edge to seal. Cut several small vents in top to allow steam to escape.

Sprinkle with sugar. Bake on bottom rack in 350°F (175°C) oven for about 50 minutes until browned and fruit is tender. Cuts into 8 wedges.

1 wedge: 389 Calories; 14.2 g Total Fat (trace Mono, 0.1 g Poly, 6.0 g Sat); 10 mg Cholesterol; 64 g Carbohydrate; 2 g Fibre; 3 g Protein; 274 mg Sodium

Pictured below.

blueberry pie

Is there nary a saskatoon berry in sight? Simply substitute an equal amount of fresh blueberries for a delicious blueberry pie.

Fresh Saskatoon Pie, page 8

A light-textured, gently sweet topping crowns a familiar dessert in a brand new way. Try it once and you'll definitely try it again and again…

Peachy Rhubarb Cobbler

Chopped fresh (or frozen, partially thawed) rhubarb	8 cups	2 L
Cans of sliced peaches in light syrup (14 oz., 398 mL, each), with syrup	2	2
Granulated sugar	1 cup	250 mL
Minute tapioca	3 tbsp.	50 mL
WALNUT BRAN TOPPING		
Butter (or hard margarine), softened	1/4 cup	60 mL
Granulated sugar	3/4 cup	175 mL
All-purpose flour	1 1/2 cups	375 mL
All-bran cereal	2/3 cup	150 mL
Chopped walnuts	1/2 cup	125 mL
Baking powder	2 tsp.	10 mL
Salt	1/4 tsp.	1 mL
Milk	1 cup	250 mL

Combine first 4 ingredients in large saucepan. Bring to a boil. Reduce heat to medium. Boil gently, uncovered, for about 7 minutes until rhubarb is tender. Spread evenly in greased 3 quart (3 L) shallow baking dish. Keep hot in 400°F (205°C) oven.

Walnut Bran Topping: Cream butter and sugar in large bowl.

Combine next 5 ingredients in medium bowl. Add half of cereal mixture to butter mixture. Stir until mixture resembles coarse crumbs.

Add milk and remaining cereal mixture. Stir until just moistened. Drop mounds of cereal mixture, using about 2 tbsp. (30 mL) for each, over hot rhubarb mixture. Bake for about 25 minutes until golden and wooden pick inserted in centre of topping comes out clean. Let stand for 10 minutes. Serves 8.

1 serving: 450 Calories; 11.4 g Total Fat (2.4 g Mono, 4.0 g Poly, 4.3 g Sat); 17 mg Cholesterol; 86 g Carbohydrate; 6 g Fibre; 7 g Protein; 216 mg Sodium

Pictured at right.

Top: Peachy Rhubarb Cobbler, above
Bottom: Strawberry Rhubarb Pie, page 8

A light dessert with a smooth filling, a sweet glaze and a fresh fruit topping. Try using both honeydew melon and cantaloupe in the topping for an eye-catching colour combination.

about cantaloupe

To avoid the cantaloupe conundrum, keep these simple shopping tips in mind when selecting your musk melon. Although a cantaloupe's colour and texture will change after being picked, all its flavour comes from being allowed to properly ripen on the vine—so you need to be on the lookout for a ripe melon. A ripe cantaloupe will have a slightly musky odour and, conversely, an odourless melon will be lacking in flavour. Another trick for testing ripeness is to push on the melon's base, opposite the stem. It should give a little without being too soft. If you find a melon that is too soft or lumpy, it really is on its last legs and will be quite watery.

Cantaloupe Flan

PASTRY		
All-purpose flour	1 cup	250 mL
Icing (confectioner's) sugar	3 tbsp.	50 mL
Cold butter (or hard margarine), cut up	1/2 cup	125 mL
Egg yolks (large)	2	2
Ice water	1 tbsp.	15 mL

FILLING		
Whipping cream	1 cup	250 mL
Chopped cantaloupe	1/2 cup	125 mL
Granulated sugar	1/2 cup	125 mL
Grated lemon zest	2 tsp.	10 mL
Envelope of unflavoured gelatin (about 1 tbsp., 15 mL)	1/4 oz.	7 g
Cold water	2 tbsp.	30 mL

TOPPING		
Large whole cantaloupe (about 1 lb., 454 g)	1	1
Apricot jam, warmed	1/4 cup	60 mL
Orange liqueur	1 tbsp.	15 mL

Pastry: Combine flour and icing sugar in medium bowl. Cut in butter until mixture resembles coarse crumbs. Beat egg yolks and ice water with fork in small bowl. Slowly add to flour mixture, stirring with fork until mixture starts to come together. Do not overmix. Turn out onto work surface. Shape into slightly flattened disc. Wrap with plastic wrap. Chill for 30 minutes. Roll out pastry on lightly floured surface to fit ungreased 8 inch (20 cm) tart pan with fluted sides and removable bottom. Carefully lift pastry and press into bottom and up side of pan. Trim edge. Place pan on ungreased baking sheet. Chill, covered, for 30 minutes. Cover pastry with parchment paper, bringing paper up over crimped edge. Fill halfway up side with dried beans. Bake on bottom rack in 375°F (190°C) oven for 20 minutes. Carefully remove paper and beans, reserving beans for next time you bake pastry. Bake shell for another 15 to 20 minutes until lightly browned. Cool.

(continued on next page)

Filling: Put first 4 ingredients into blender or food processor. Process until smooth. Transfer to medium bowl.

Sprinkle gelatin over cold water in small saucepan. Let stand for 1 minute. Heat and stir on low until gelatin is dissolved. Add to whipping cream mixture. Stir well. Pour into crust. Chill for 2 to 3 hours until set.

Topping: Scoop balls from cantaloupe using small melon baller. Arrange in single layer over whipping cream mixture.

Combine jam and liqueur in small bowl. Brush over cantaloupe. Chill. Cuts into 6 wedges.

1 wedge: 520 Calories; 31.0 g Total Fat (8.7 g Mono, 1.4 g Poly, 18.8 g Sat); 154 mg Cholesterol; 58 g Carbohydrate; 2 g Fibre; 5 g Protein; 157 mg Sodium

Pictured below.

Sweet as the sun on a summer day, this light and lovely shortcake will raise the spirits of all who taste it!

variations

Strawberry's not the only fruit in town. Try using an equal amount of fresh raspberries or mashed or sliced fresh peaches.

Strawberry Shortcake

Package of white cake mix (1 layer size)	1	1
Fresh strawberries	4 cups	1 L
Granulated sugar	3 tbsp.	50 mL
Whipping cream	1 cup	250 mL
Granulated sugar	1 tbsp.	15 mL
Vanilla extract	1/2 tsp.	2 mL

Prepare cake mix according to package directions in 9 inch (22 cm) round cake pan. Cool. Cut in half horizontally. Set aside.

Mash strawberries and first amount of sugar in large bowl. Place 1 layer of cake, cut-side up, on serving plate. Spread half of strawberry mixture over cake. Place remaining layer of cake, cut-side down, over top. Spread remaining strawberry mixture over cake. Chill, covered, until ready to serve.

Beat remaining 3 ingredients in medium bowl until soft peaks form. Spread over top of cake. Cuts into 8 wedges.

1 wedge: 544 Calories; 24.4 g Total Fat (9.0 g Mono, 4.0 g Poly, 10.1 g Sat); 40 mg Cholesterol; 77 g Carbohydrate; 3 g Fibre; 7 g Protein; 374 mg Sodium

A touch of orange liqueur gives that little something extra to the filling of these luscious strawberry layers delicately nestled between puff pastry.

Strawberry Cream Layers

Package of puff pastry (14 oz., 397 g), thawed according to package directions	1/2	1/2
Chopped fresh strawberries	1 1/2 cups	375 mL
Strawberry jam, warmed	1/3 cup	75 mL
Icing (confectioner's) sugar	1/4 cup	60 mL
Orange liqueur	2 tbsp.	30 mL
Whipping cream	1 cup	250 mL
Icing (confectioner's) sugar, sprinkle		

Melted pink candy melting wafers, for garnish
Melted chocolate melting wafers, for garnish

(continued on next page)

Roll out pastry on lightly floured surface to 12 inch (30 cm) square. Place on greased baking sheet. Grease outside bottom of separate baking sheet. Place directly on top of pastry. Bake in 450°F (230°C) oven for 15 to 20 minutes until golden. Remove pastry from baking sheet and place on wire rack to cool. Cut into 12 rectangles.

Combine next 4 ingredients in large bowl. Chill, covered, for 30 minutes. Drain, reserving syrup.

Beat whipping cream in small bowl until soft peaks form. Fold in strawberry mixture. Place 1 pastry rectangle on baking sheet. Top with 6 tbsp. (100 mL) filling. Place another pastry rectangle over filling. Top with 6 tbsp. (100 mL) filling. Place third pastry rectangle over filling. Repeat with remaining pastry rectangles and filling to make 4 stacks. Sprinkle tops with icing sugar.

Garnish 4 individual serving plates with melted pink and chocolate wafers and reserved syrup. Carefully place 1 stack on each plate. Serves 4.

1 serving: 609 Calories; 39.9 g Total Fat (16.8 g Mono, 3.3 g Poly, 17.8 g Sat); 76 mg Cholesterol; 57 g Carbohydrate; 2 g Fibre; 5 g Protein; 146 mg Sodium

Pictured below.

about melting wafers

Melting wafers are made from a special variety of chocolate that is specifically designed to be melted and used to make candies and other desserts. The most common types are milk chocolate, dark chocolate and white chocolate-flavoured—although you can often find the white variety dyed to almost any colour under the rainbow. You can purchase melting wafers at specialty kitchen or craft stores, but many supermarkets also carry them in bulk.

Strawberry Cream Layers, page 14

Dumplings get a sweet new twist when they're slow cooked atop a delicious stew of rhubarb, strawberries, blueberries and raspberries.

Berry Rhubarb Dumpling Dessert

Chopped fresh (or frozen, thawed) rhubarb	2 cups	500 mL
Fresh (or frozen, whole) strawberries, sliced	1 1/3 cups	325 mL
Fresh (or frozen) blueberries	1 1/3 cups	325 mL
Fresh (or frozen, whole) raspberries	1 1/3 cups	325 mL
Granulated sugar	3/4 cup	175 mL
Cornstarch	4 tsp.	20 mL
DUMPLINGS		
All-purpose flour	1 1/2 cups	375 mL
Granulated sugar	2 tbsp.	30 mL
Baking powder	1 tbsp.	15 mL
Salt	1/2 tsp.	2 mL
Milk	2/3 cup	150 mL
Butter (or hard margarine), melted	1/4 cup	60 mL
Vanilla extract	1 tsp.	5 mL

Layer first 4 ingredients, in order given, in 3 1/2 quart (3.5 L) slow cooker.

Combine sugar and cornstarch in small bowl. Sprinkle over fruit. Cook, covered, on High for 1 1/2 hours. Stir.

Dumplings: Measure first 4 ingredients into medium bowl. Stir. Make a well in centre.

Combine remaining 3 ingredients in small bowl. Add to well. Stir until soft dough forms. Spoon 8 mounds of batter over fruit mixture. Cook, covered, on High for about 30 minutes until wooden pick inserted into centre of dumpling comes out clean. Serves 8.

1 serving: 264 Calories; 6.2 g Total Fat (1.6 g Mono, 0.4 g Poly, 3.8 g Sat); 16 mg Cholesterol; 50 g Carbohydrate; 3 g Fibre; 4 g Protein; 297 mg Sodium

Pictured at right.

food fun

There are two different beverages called "cordial"—a high-alcohol liqueur, and a concentrated, non-alcoholic syrup that is used in mixed drinks and desserts. Lime cordial, the non-alcoholic mixture of lime juice and sugar used in Tropical Trifle, is available in many supermarkets. Because of its sweetness, it should never be used as a substitute for lime juice, but it's great in mixed drinks—try mixing with soda water (and, if so inclined, a shot of vodka) and serving over ice for a tangy, refreshing summer beverage.

Tropical Trifle

CUSTARD		
Custard powder	1/4 cup	60 mL
Granulated sugar	1/4 cup	60 mL
Milk	2 cups	500 mL
Grated orange zest	1 tsp.	5 mL
CARAMEL SAUCE		
Brown sugar, packed	1/2 cup	125 mL
Butter (or hard margarine), cut up	1/2 cup	125 mL
Whipping cream	1/2 cup	125 mL
TRIFLE		
Pineapple juice	1/2 cup	125 mL
Lime cordial	1/4 cup	60 mL
Tequila	1/4 cup	60 mL
Frozen pound cakes (10 1/2 oz., 298 g, each), thawed and cut into 1/2 inch (12 mm) cubes	2	2
Halved fresh strawberries	1 1/2 cups	375 mL
Kiwifruit, sliced	4	4
Can of mandarin orange segments, drained	10 oz.	284 mL

Kiwifruit slices, for garnish
Quartered fresh strawberries, for garnish

Custard: Combine custard powder and granulated sugar in medium saucepan. Stir in milk. Add orange zest. Heat and stir on medium until boiling and thickened. Pour into medium bowl. Chill, covered, for about 1 hour, stirring occasionally, until slightly cooled. Makes about 2 cups (500 mL) custard.

Caramel Sauce: Combine all 3 ingredients in separate medium saucepan. Heat and stir on medium for about 5 minutes until boiling and butter is melted. Boil gently, uncovered, for about 5 minutes, without stirring, until slightly thickened. Transfer to separate medium bowl. Chill, covered, for about 1 hour, stirring occasionally, until slightly cooled. Makes about 1 1/3 cups (325 mL) sauce.

Trifle: Combine first 3 ingredients in medium shallow dish. Dip cake cubes in pineapple juice mixture.

(continued on next page)

To assemble, layer ingredients in 10 cup (2.5 L) glass trifle bowl as follows:

1. 1/3 of cake cubes
2. Stand strawberries around edge, cut-side out
3. 1/2 of custard
4. 1/3 of cake cubes
5. Caramel Sauce
6. Place kiwifruit slices around edge, cut-side out
7. Remaining cake cubes
8. Remaining custard
9. Mandarin orange segments

Garnish with kiwifruit and strawberries. Chill for at least 8 hours or overnight. Makes about 10 cups (2.5 L). Serves 8.

1 serving: 665 Calories; 32.8 g Total Fat (4.9 g Mono, 0.8 g Poly, 19.6 g Sat); 236 mg Cholesterol; 83 g Carbohydrate; 2 g Fibre; 8 g Protein; 457 mg Sodium

Pictured below.

Our tempting filling takes the tortilla from everyday supper fare to a fabulously festive dessert.

Fruity Tortillas

Fresh raspberries	2/3 cup	150 mL
Fresh (or frozen, thawed) blueberries	1/3 cup	75 mL
Sliced fresh strawberries	1/3 cup	75 mL
1% cottage cheese	1/4 cup	60 mL
Skim milk	4 tsp.	20 mL
Granulated sugar	1 tsp.	5 mL
Lemon juice	3/4 tsp.	4 mL
Flour tortillas (6 inch, 15 cm, diameter), warmed	8	8

Put first 3 ingredients into small bowl. Toss gently.

Put next 4 ingredients into blender. Process until smooth.

Fold tortilla in half, then in half again. Lift 1 side to form a hollow. Spoon about 2 1/2 tbsp. (37 mL) fruit mixture into hollow. Holding tortilla upright, drizzle about 2 tsp. (10 mL) cottage cheese mixture over fruit, allowing mixture to run down through fruit. Repeat with remaining tortillas, fruit and cottage cheese mixture. Makes 8 tortillas.

1 tortilla: 109 Calories; 3.2 g Total Fat (trace Mono, trace Poly, trace Sat); trace Cholesterol; 16 g Carbohydrate; 1 g Fibre; 4 g Protein; 254 mg Sodium

Pictured at right.

Top: Fruity Tortillas, above
Bottom: Apple Cream Quesadillas, page 22

If you like Danish pastry but not the calories that go with it, try this one on for size! It's an apple and sweet cream dream.

banana quesadillas

For a completely different flavour sensation, omit the apples and use 1 cup (250 mL) of diced banana instead.

Apple Cream Quesadillas

Light cream cheese, softened	4 oz.	125 g
Brown sugar, packed	2 tbsp.	30 mL
Vanilla extract	1/2 tsp.	2 mL
Finely diced unpeeled red apple	1 cup	250 mL
Flour tortillas (9 inch, 22 cm, diameter)	4	4
Ground cinnamon, sprinkle		

Preheat gas barbecue to medium. Mash cream cheese with fork in small bowl. Add brown sugar and vanilla. Mix well.

Sprinkle apple over 2 tortillas. Sprinkle with cinnamon. Spread cream cheese mixture evenly over remaining tortillas, almost to edge. Place, cream cheese-side down, over apple. Press down gently. Carefully transfer quesadillas to greased grill. Cook for 1 to 2 minutes until grill marks appear. Carefully turn over. Cook for 1 to 2 minutes until crispy. Let stand for 1 minute. Each quesadilla cuts into 4 wedges, for a total of 8 wedges.

1 wedge: 118 Calories; 4.2 g Total Fat (0 g Mono, 0 g Poly, 2.1 g Sat); 6.6 mg Cholesterol; 17 g Carbohydrate; trace Fibre; 3 g Protein; 223 mg Sodium

Pictured on page 21.

With colour on a grand scale, this no-fuss dessert makes the most of fresh, in-season peaches, although canned peaches will do, too. Ideal for those lazy late-summer days.

Poached Peaches In Raspberry Sauce

Fresh peaches (see Tip, page 23)	8	8
Boiling water	9 cups	2.25 L
RASPBERRY SAUCE		
Fresh (or frozen, thawed) raspberries	3 cups	750 mL
Icing (confectioner's) sugar	1/4 cup	60 mL
Raspberry (or orange) liqueur	1/4 cup	60 mL
Sliced almonds, toasted (see Tip, page 48)	1/3 cup	75 mL

Add peaches to boiling water in large saucepan. Simmer for 5 minutes. Transfer with slotted spoon to large bowl of ice water. Let stand for 10 minutes. Peel. Cut in half. Remove and discard pits.

(continued on next page)

Raspberry Sauce: Put all 3 ingredients into blender or food processor. Process until almost smooth. Strain through sieve into small bowl. Discard seeds. Makes about 1 2/3 cups (400 mL) sauce. Place peach halves in 8 individual serving bowls. Drizzle with Raspberry Sauce.

Sprinkle with almonds. Serves 8.

1 serving: 138 Calories; 3.3 g Total Fat (1.9 g Mono, 0.9 g Poly, 0.2 g Sat); 0 mg Cholesterol; 24 g Carbohydrate; 6 g Fibre; 3 g Protein; 3 mg Sodium

Pictured below.

tip

When cooking with fruit, choose produce that is fresh and unblemished. As fruit heats, it softens and overripe or bruised fruit may become quite mushy.

1. Vanilla Bean Fruit Salad, page 24
2. Strawberries In Almond Liqueur, page 25
3. Poached Peaches In Raspberry Sauce, page 22

The ancient Aztecs of Mexico were the first keepers of the secrets of vanilla. Now we all know how wonderful it is, especially in this remarkable fruit salad.

about vanilla

You'll never catch us using the term "plain vanilla"—we feel that this familiar, yet exotic, flavour deserves more respect! Vanilla beans come from the only tropical orchid that bears an edible fruit. The beans gain their characteristic flavour only after they are sun-dried and fermented. Because the process is fairly labour-intensive, vanilla beans and true vanilla extract can be a bit pricey—although imitation vanilla extract can be used in a pinch.

Vanilla Bean Fruit Salad

VANILLA SYRUP		
Granulated sugar	1 cup	250 mL
Water	1/2 cup	125 mL
Vanilla bean	1	1
Grated lime zest	1/2 tsp.	2 mL
SALAD		
Cubed fresh pineapple	5 cups	1.25 L
Cubed cantaloupe	2 cups	500 mL
Kiwifruit, quartered	4	4
Quartered fresh strawberries	3 cups	750 mL
Sparkling white (or rosé) wine (or white grape juice)	1/2 cup	125 mL
Fresh mint leaves, torn	12	12

Sprigs of fresh mint, for garnish

Vanilla Syrup: Combine sugar and water in small saucepan. Split vanilla bean in half lengthwise. Scrape seeds from pod into sugar mixture. Add pod halves. Heat and stir on medium for about 4 minutes until sugar is dissolved. Increase heat to medium-high. Brush side of saucepan with wet pastry brush to dissolve any sugar crystals. Boil for about 5 minutes, without stirring, until slightly thickened. Remove from heat.

Add lime zest. Stir. Let stand for 10 minutes. Pour into extra-large bowl. Chill, covered, for 1 hour. Remove and discard pod halves. Leave seeds in syrup. Makes about 1 cup (250 mL) syrup.

Salad: Add first 3 ingredients to syrup. Stir until coated. Chill, covered, for at least 3 hours, stirring occasionally.

Add next 3 ingredients. Stir. Spoon into 8 dessert bowls.

Garnish individual servings with mint sprigs. Makes about 9 1/2 cups (2.4 L). Serves 8.

1 serving: 207 Calories; 0.6 g Total Fat (0.1 g Mono, 0.3 g Poly, 0.1 g Sat); 0 mg Cholesterol; 50 g Carbohydrate; 4 g Fibre; 2 g Protein; 10 mg Sodium

Pictured on page 23.

Strawberries In Almond Liqueur

Sliced fresh strawberries	2 cups	500 mL
Almond liqueur	1/4 cup	60 mL
Vanilla ice cream	1 cup	250 mL

Combine strawberries and liqueur in medium bowl. Let stand, covered, at room temperature for 3 hours, stirring occasionally.

Scoop ice cream into 4 small serving bowls. Spoon strawberry mixture over top. Serves 4.

1 serving: 212 Calories; 9.3 g Total Fat (trace Mono, 0.2 g Poly, 5.5 g Sat); 60 mg Cholesterol; 23 g Carbohydrate; 2 g Fibre; 3 g Protein; 37 mg Sodium

Pictured on page 23.

This super-simple dessert of marinated strawberries over ice cream has a decadence that'll make your guests feel truly treasured. Remember to allow enough time to let the strawberries properly marinate.

Drunken Watermelon

Bottles of lemon vodka cooler (11 1/2 oz., 330 mL, each)	4	4
Orange liqueur	2/3 cup	150 mL
Medium watermelon	1/2	1/2

Combine coolers and liqueur in extra-large bowl.

Cut watermelon crosswise into 3/4 inch (2 cm) thick slices. Cut each slice into 8 wedges. Layer wedges in liqueur mixture. Turn gently until coated. Chill, covered, for at least 6 hours or overnight, turning occasionally. Serves 10.

1 serving: 209 Calories; 0.4 g Total Fat (0.1 g Mono, 0.1 g Poly, 0.1 g Sat); 0 mg Cholesterol; 36 g Carbohydrate; 1 g Fibre; 1 g Protein; 3 mg Sodium

Pictured on page 31.

This lemon vodka and orange liqueur-soaked watermelon is a sure-fire summer party favourite. (Feel free to sip away at the leftover watermelon and cooler mixture!)

Whether you want an impressive fancy-pants dessert or an easy, everyday top-off to a family meal, this one is it.

kiwi with orange custard

An often overlooked combination, kiwifruit and orange actually suit each other very well. To give it a go, omit the strawberries and use an equal amount of sliced kiwi.

Strawberries With Orange Custard

Icing (confectioner's) sugar	2 tbsp.	30 mL
Orange liqueur (or orange juice)	2 tbsp.	30 mL
Thickly sliced fresh strawberries	6 cups	1.5 L
ORANGE CUSTARD		
Granulated sugar	1/2 cup	125 mL
All-purpose flour	1 tbsp.	15 mL
Cornstarch	1 tbsp.	15 mL
Milk	1 1/2 cups	375 mL
Egg yolks (large)	2	2
Grated orange zest	2 tsp.	10 mL

Combine icing sugar and liqueur in medium bowl. Add strawberries. Stir gently. Chill, covered, for 1 hour.

Orange Custard: Combine first 3 ingredients in medium saucepan. Slowly add milk, stirring constantly, until smooth. Heat and stir on medium for about 10 minutes until boiling and thickened.

Beat egg yolks with fork in small bowl. Add 3 tbsp. (50 mL) hot milk mixture, stirring constantly. Add to remaining hot milk mixture. Heat and stir until boiling and thickened.

Add orange zest. Stir. Transfer to small bowl. Cover with plastic wrap directly on surface to prevent skin from forming. Chill for about 3 hours until cold. Makes about 1 2/3 cups (400 mL) custard. Spoon strawberry mixture into 4 individual serving bowls. Spoon custard over top. Serves 4.

1 serving: 276 Calories; 4.2 g Total Fat (1.6 g Mono, 0.8 g Poly, 1.4 g Sat); 110 mg Cholesterol; 56 g Carbohydrate; 5 g Fibre; 7 g Protein; 55 mg Sodium

Pictured at right.

1. Blueberries Romanoff, page 29
2. Strawberries With Orange Custard, above
3. Peach Melba Sundaes, page 28

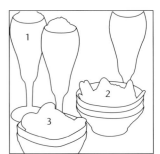

Melon Banana Splits

Large bananas, halved crosswise	2	2
Chopped cantaloupe	1 1/3 cups	325 mL
Chopped honeydew	1 1/3 cups	325 mL
Chopped watermelon	1 1/3 cups	325 mL
Vanilla yogurt	1 cup	250 mL
Chopped fresh pineapple (or canned tidbits, drained)	1/4 cup	60 mL
Fresh blueberries	1/4 cup	60 mL
Fresh raspberries	1/4 cup	60 mL
Caramel ice cream topping (optional)	2 tbsp.	30 mL

Cut banana halves lengthwise to make 8 pieces. Place 2 banana pieces on opposite sides of 4 banana split dishes or shallow bowls.

Drop spoonfuls of next 3 ingredients in separate mounds between banana pieces.

Drizzle yogurt over melon.

Sprinkle next 3 ingredients over yogurt.

Drizzle with ice cream topping. Serves 4.

1 serving: 161 Calories; 1.3 g Total Fat (trace Mono, 0.2 g Poly, 0.6 g Sat); 4 mg Cholesterol; 37 g Carbohydrate; 4 g Fibre; 4 g Protein; 61 mg Sodium

Peach Melba Sundaes

MELBA SAUCE		
Container of frozen raspberries in syrup, thawed	15 oz.	425 g
Cornstarch	1 tbsp.	15 mL
Water	2 tbsp.	30 mL
SUNDAE		
Fresh peaches, cut into 10 slices each	2	2
Granulated sugar	1 tbsp.	15 mL
Vanilla ice cream	1 cup	250 mL

(continued on next page)

Melba Sauce: Drain raspberry syrup into small saucepan. Put raspberries into small bowl. Bring syrup to a boil on medium.

Stir cornstarch into water in small cup. Add to syrup. Heat and stir until boiling and thickened. Remove from heat. Mash raspberries. Add to syrup. Stir. Cool. Makes about 1 2/3 cups (400 mL) sauce.

Sundae: Put peach slices and sugar into medium bowl. Toss until coated. Scoop ice cream into 4 individual serving bowls. Arrange peach slices over ice cream. Top with Melba Sauce. Serves 4.

1 serving: 347 Calories; 9.0 g Total Fat (0 g Mono, 0 g Poly, 5.5 g Sat); 60 mg Cholesterol; 63 g Carbohydrate; 4 g Fibre; 4 g Protein; 61 mg Sodium

Pictured on page 27.

Blueberries Romanoff

Fresh blueberries	4 cups	1 L
Icing (confectioners) sugar	1/2 cup	125 mL
Orange juice	1/2 cup	125 mL
Orange liqueur	1 tsp.	5 mL
Whipping cream	1 cup	250 mL
Granulated sugar	1 tbsp.	15 mL
Orange liqueur	1 tsp.	5 mL

Combine first 4 ingredients in large bowl. Chill, covered, for 2 hours, stirring occasionally.

Beat whipping cream and sugar in medium bowl until soft peaks form. Add second amount of liqueur. Stir. Spoon berry mixture into 8 tall glasses. Spoon whipped cream mixture over top. Serves 8.

1 serving: 186 Calories; 10.7 g Total Fat (3.1 g Mono, 0.5 g Poly, 6.5 g Sat); 38 mg Cholesterol; 23 g Carbohydrate; 2 g Fibre; 1 g Protein; 12 mg Sodium

Pictured on page 27.

It's gotta be fresh fruit for sure. This very impressive, yet uncomplicated dessert just screams "high society," especially if served in champagne glasses.

variations

This recipe is especially well-suited to apricots, peaches or strawberries. Whatever your fancy, just exchange the blueberries for an equal amount of the fresh fruit of your choice.

Fresh fruit marinated in traditional margarita flavours is a great way to either start off or finish up any adults-only barbecue.

Margaritagrill

Brown sugar, packed	1/4 cup	60 mL
Orange liqueur	1/4 cup	60 mL
Tequila	1/4 cup	60 mL
Lemon juice	1 tbsp.	15 mL
Lime juice	1 tbsp.	15 mL
Grated lemon zest	1 tsp.	5 mL
Grated lime zest	1 tsp.	5 mL
Medium nectarines (or peaches), cut into 6 wedges each	2	2
Slightly green bananas, sliced diagonally	2	2
Large orange, peeled and sliced crosswise	1	1
Medium unpeeled cooking apple (such as McIntosh), cored and sliced into rings	1	1

Preheat gas barbecue to high. Stir first 7 ingredients in small bowl until brown sugar is dissolved.

Put remaining 4 ingredients into large bowl. Add tequila mixture. Stir. Let stand at room temperature for 30 minutes. Drain and discard tequila mixture. Cook fruit on greased grill for about 1 minute per side until golden. Serves 6.

1 serving: 162 Calories; 0.4 g Total Fat (trace Mono, 0.1 g Poly, 0.1 g Sat); 0 mg Cholesterol; 32 g Carbohydrate; 3 g Fibre; 1 g Protein; 4 mg Sodium

Pictured at right.

1. Drunken Watermelon, page 25
2. Margaritagrill, above
3. Marshmallow Fruit Kabobs, page 32
4. Grilled Pineapple Chunks, page 32
5. Grilled Peaches, page 33

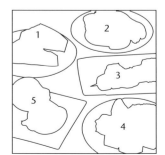

broiled pineapple chunks

Not barbecue weather? Arrange pineapple on a greased broiler pan, and broil on the top oven rack for five minutes per side until browned. Remember to brush liberally with the syrup mixture throughout.

Grilled Pineapple Chunks

Maple (or maple-flavoured) syrup	1/4 cup	60 mL
Butter (or hard margarine)	3 tbsp.	50 mL
Granulated sugar	3 tbsp.	50 mL
Orange liqueur	3 tbsp.	50 mL
Ground nutmeg	1/2 tsp.	2 mL
Large fresh pineapple, peeled, quartered lengthwise, core removed	1	1
ORANGE MASCARPONE SAUCE		
Package of mascarpone cheese, softened	10 1/2 oz.	275 g
Icing (confectioner's) sugar	2 tbsp.	30 mL
Orange liqueur	2 tbsp.	30 mL
Grated orange zest	1/2 tsp.	2 mL

Combine first 5 ingredients in medium saucepan. Heat and stir on low for 10 to 12 minutes until butter is melted.

Brush pineapple quarters with syrup mixture. Preheat gas barbecue to medium. Cook pineapple on greased grill for about 5 minutes per side, brushing with syrup mixture, until browned. Transfer to large plate. Cut pineapple quarters crosswise into 1 1/2 inch (3.8 cm) pieces.

Orange Mascarpone Sauce: Combine all 4 ingredients in small bowl. Makes about 1 cup (250 mL) sauce. Serve with pineapple. Serves 6.

1 serving: 411 Calories; 26.9 g Total Fat (1.5 g Mono, 0.3 g Poly, 16.1 g Sat); 77 mg Cholesterol; 33 g Carbohydrate; 1 g Fibre; 4 g Protein; 70 mg Sodium

Pictured on page 31.

The marshmallows will remind you of your campfire days, and the ripe, grilled fruit will make new memories all the sweeter.

Marshmallow Fruit Kabobs

Medium banana, cut into 8 pieces	1	1
Chunks of fresh pineapple (1 1/2 inches, 3.8 cm, each)	8	8
Large marshmallows	8	8
Bamboo skewers (8 inches, 20 cm, each), soaked in water for 10 minutes	4	4
Butter (or hard margarine), melted	1 tbsp.	15 mL

(continued on next page)

Thread first 3 ingredients alternately onto skewers.

Brush with butter. Preheat gas barbecue to medium. Cook skewers on greased grill for about 1 minute per side until marshmallows start to soften and brown. Makes 4 kabobs.

1 kabob: 102 Calories; 3.0 g Total Fat (0.8 g Mono, 0.1 g Poly, 1.8 g Sat); 8 mg Cholesterol; 20 g Carbohydrate; 1 g Fibre; 1 g Protein; 27 mg Sodium

Pictured on page 31.

Grilled Peaches

Balsamic vinegar	1/4 cup	60 mL
Liquid honey	2 tbsp.	30 mL
Olive (or canola) oil	2 tsp.	10 mL
Finely chopped fresh mint (or 3/4 tsp., 4 mL, dried)	1 tbsp.	15 mL
Fresh peaches, halved (or 8 canned peach halves)	4	4
Frozen whipped topping, thawed (optional)	1/2 cup	125 mL
Chopped fresh mint, for garnish		

Preheat gas barbecue to medium-high. Whisk first 3 ingredients in large bowl. Add mint. Stir.

Add peach halves. Toss until coated. Place peaches on greased grill, cut-side down. Close lid. Cook for 6 to 8 minutes, turning once and brushing with balsamic mixture, until peaches are tender but still hold their shape. Arrange peaches on 4 dessert plates.

Spoon whipped topping over peaches.

Garnish with mint. Serves 4.

1 serving: 104 Calories; 2.3 g Total Fat (1.7 g Mono, 0.2 g Poly, 0.3 g Sat); 0 mg Cholesterol; 21 g Carbohydrate; 2 g Fibre; 1 g Protein; 5 mg Sodium

Pictured on page 31.

Balsamic vinegar and honey caramelize to form a tangy and sweet coating on tender peaches. Your guests will grill you for the recipe.

Grilled fruit is the perfect sweet treat. In this recipe, the addition of a sugary syrup makes these kabobs out of this world!

Fruit Kabobs

Fresh strawberry pieces	12	12
Kiwifruit pieces	12	12
Pound cake cubes	12	12
Cantaloupe cubes	6	6
Bamboo skewers (8 inches, 20 cm, each), soaked in water for 10 minutes	6	6
Granulated sugar	1 cup	250 mL
Water	1 cup	250 mL
Cornstarch	2 tbsp.	30 mL

Thread first 4 ingredients alternately onto skewers.

Combine remaining 3 ingredients in small saucepan. Heat and stir on medium until boiling and thickened. Brush on skewers. Preheat gas barbecue to medium. Cook skewers on greased grill for about 5 minutes, turning occasionally and brushing with sugar mixture, until grill marks appear. Makes 6 kabobs.

1 kabob: 387 Calories; 11.5 g Total Fat (3.4 g Mono, 0.7 g Poly, 6.6 g Sat); 125 mg Cholesterol; 70 g Carbohydrate; 2 g Fibre; 4 g Protein; 232 mg Sodium

Pictured at right.

This dip works well with any flavour of yogurt. It is mild, creamy and fresh tasting. Use as a dip for fresh fruit or spoon over your favourite dessert. Fast and easy to prepare.

Yogurt Fruit Dip

Strawberry yogurt	1/2 cup	125 mL
Icing (confectioner's) sugar	1 tbsp.	15 mL
Frozen whipped topping, thawed	1/2 cup	125 mL

Fold yogurt and icing sugar into whipped topping in small bowl. Makes about 3/4 cup (175 mL).

2 tbsp. (30 mL): 41 Calories; 1.5 g Total Fat (0 g Mono, 0 g Poly, 1.5 g Sat); 1 mg Cholesterol; 6 g Carbohydrate; 0 g Fibre; 1 g Protein; 16 mg Sodium

Pictured at right.

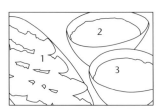

1. Fruit Kabobs, above
2. Cool Fruit Dip, page 35
3. Yogurt Fruit Dip, above

Cool Fruit Dip

Marshmallow creme	3/4 cup	175 mL
Sour cream	1/2 cup	125 mL
Brown sugar, packed	1 tbsp.	15 mL
Vanilla extract	1/2 tsp.	2 mL
Frozen whipped topping, thawed (or 1 envelope of dessert topping, prepared)	2 cups	500 mL

This creamy, fluffy dip adds a touch of fun and refreshment to an everyday fruit platter. Serve with any fruit that strikes your fancy.

Beat first 4 ingredients in medium bowl until brown sugar is dissolved and mixture is smooth.

Fold in whipped topping. Makes about 2 1/2 cups (625 mL).

2 tbsp. (30 mL): 44 Calories; 2.5 g Total Fat (0.3 g Mono, trace Poly, 2.1 g Sat); 2 mg Cholesterol; 5 g Carbohydrate; 0 g Fibre; trace Protein; 10 mg Sodium

Pictured below.

food fun

There is much debate over who originally created this decadent dessert of crisp meringue filled with whipped cream and fresh fruit. Both New Zealander and Australian gourmands hotly contest the issue on a regular basis. The only thing they do agree on is who the dessert was named after—beautiful Russian dancer Anna Pavlowa (the w is pronounced as a v), who visited both regions in the 1920s. A fitting tribute to a dancer who, like the dessert, seemed to be as light as air.

Pavlova

MERINGUE		
Egg whites (large), room temperature	4	4
Granulated sugar	1 cup	250 mL
White vinegar	1 tsp.	5 mL
TOPPING		
Whipping cream	1 1/2 cups	375 mL
Halved fresh strawberries	1 1/2 cups	375 mL
Kiwifruit, halved lengthwise and sliced	2	2

Meringue: Line bottom of baking sheet with parchment (not waxed) paper. Trace one 7 inch (18 cm) circle on paper. Turn paper over. Beat egg whites in large bowl until soft peaks form. Add sugar, 1 tbsp. (15 mL) at a time, beating constantly until stiff peaks form and sugar is dissolved.

Fold in vinegar. Spoon onto circle. Spread evenly to edge of circle. Using knife, shape edge of circle up towards centre to make decorative pattern. Bake on bottom rack in 225°F (110°C) oven for about 2 hours until dry. Turn oven off. Let stand in oven until cool.

Topping: Beat whipping cream in medium bowl until soft peaks form. Carefully cut circle in top of meringue, 1 inch (2.5 cm) from edge, using small sharp knife. Lightly press circle down to sink top slightly. Spoon whipped cream onto meringue.

Arrange strawberries and kiwifruit over whipped cream. Cuts into 10 wedges.

1 wedge: 216 Calories; 12.7 g Total Fat (3.7 g Mono, 0.5 g Poly, 7.8 g Sat); 46 mg Cholesterol; 25 g Carbohydrate; 1 g Fibre; 3 g Protein; 35 mg Sodium

Pictured on front cover and at right.

A heavenly cake! The burnt sugar syrup gives it a caramel taste that is beyond compare. Add some flair to this dessert by serving with whipped cream and caramelized sugar.

tip

So what are you supposed to do with all the leftover egg yolks after you've separated out the whites? You could use them in a hollandaise or Béarnaise sauce or, better yet, use them in Vanilla Coconut Ice Cream, page 112. Or if you want to forgo the yolks altogether, simply use egg white product instead and follow the conversion on the package.

tip

Store remaining syrup in jar with tight-fitting lid at room temperature for up to 6 months.

Burnt Sugar Angel Food

BURNT SUGAR SYRUP		
Granulated sugar	1 cup	250 mL
Boiling water	1/2 cup	125 mL
ANGEL FOOD CAKE		
Sifted cake flour	1 cup	250 mL
Icing (confectioner's) sugar	1/2 cup	125 mL
Egg whites (large), room temperature	12	12
Cream of tartar	1 1/2 tsp.	7 mL
Salt	1/4 tsp.	1 mL
Granulated sugar	1 cup	250 mL
Vanilla extract	1 tsp.	5 mL
Maple extract	1/4 tsp.	1 mL

Burnt Sugar Syrup: Measure granulated sugar into large heavy saucepan. Heat and stir on medium for about 10 minutes until sugar is dissolved. Brush side of saucepan with wet pastry brush to dissolve any sugar crystals. Simmer for about 2 minutes, without stirring, until dark butterscotch colour. Remove from heat.

Slowly and carefully add boiling water. Sugar mixture will sputter furiously. Return to heat. Stir for about 2 minutes until smooth. Colour should be deep golden brown. Let stand for about 1 hour until cooled completely. Makes about 3/4 cup (175 mL) syrup.

Angel Food Cake: Sift flour and icing sugar together 3 times onto sheets of waxed paper or separate bowls. Set aside.

Beat next 3 ingredients in large bowl until soft peaks form. Add granulated sugar, 1/4 cup (60 mL) at a time, beating constantly until stiff peaks form and sugar is dissolved.

Add vanilla, maple extract and 3 tbsp. (50 mL) Burnt Sugar Syrup (see Tip). Beat until just combined. Sift flour mixture over egg white mixture in 4 parts, folding after each addition until just blended. Spread in ungreased 10 inch (25 cm) angel food tube pan. Cut through batter gently with knife to remove air pockets. Bake in 375°F (190°C) oven for 35 to 40 minutes until wooden pick inserted in centre of cake comes out clean. Invert cake in pan onto glass bottle for about 1 hour until cooled completely (see Tip, page 40). Turn upright. Run knife around inside edge of pan to loosen cake. Remove bottom of pan with cake. Run knife around tube and bottom of pan to loosen cake. Invert onto large serving plate. Cuts into 16 wedges.

(continued on next page)

1 wedge: 147 Calories; 0.1 g Total Fat (trace Mono, trace Poly, trace Sat); 0 mg Cholesterol; 34 g Carbohydrate; 0 g Fibre; 3 g Protein; 78 mg Sodium

Pictured on page 41.

Lemon Coconut Angel

Angel food cake (10 inch, 25 cm, diameter)	1	1
Can of lemon pie filling	19 oz.	540 mL
Medium unsweetened coconut, toasted (see Tip, page 48)	1/2 cup	125 mL
Frozen whipped topping, thawed (or whipped cream)	2 cups	500 mL
Medium unsweetened coconut, toasted (see Tip, page 48)	1/2 cup	125 mL

Cut cake horizontally into 3 layers. Place largest, bottom layer, cut-side up, on large serving plate.

Transfer 1/2 cup (125 mL) pie filling to small bowl. Set aside. Put remaining pie filling into separate small bowl. Add first amount of coconut. Stir. Spread half of coconut mixture on bottom cake layer. Place centre cake layer over coconut mixture. Spread remaining coconut mixture over centre layer. Cover with smallest, top cake layer, cut-side down.

Fold whipped topping into reserved pie filling. Spread over top and side of cake.

Sprinkle with second amount of coconut. Chill for about 1 hour until filling is firm. Cuts into 12 wedges.

1 wedge: 358 Calories; 9.8 g Total Fat (1.5 g Mono, 0.8 g Poly, 7.0 g Sat); 59 mg Cholesterol; 65 g Carbohydrate; 1 g Fibre; 6 g Protein; 358 mg Sodium

Pictured on page 41.

An attractive, layered angel food cake filled with sweet lemon and toasty coconut. It's as easy as it is delicious.

tip

The best way to cut angel food cake is to use a serrated knife and a gentle sawing motion, wiping the blade clean after each cut.

We think chiffon is kind of like a ballet—soft, weightless, easy—which describes this chiffon cake perfectly. Whipped cream and orange zest make the perfect topping for this light-tasting dessert.

tip

In our recipes we tell you to invert your angel food cake pan over a glass bottle to let it cool. This is to ensure the cake doesn't touch the counter while it's cooling. Using a bottle is only necessary if your pan does not have "feet" that keep the cake surface elevated off the counter.

about cake flour

It may not be a coincidence that "flour" and "flower" sound so much alike—the English word "flour" actually comes from the French *fleur de farine*, meaning "flower of the wheat." Cake flour is one of the finest-textured of flours, and its high starch content results in light and delicate desserts. If you don't have cake flour, you can substitute regular flour—just remove 2 tbsp (30 mL) of all-purpose flour for every 1 cup (250 mL) of cake flour that's called for.

Orange Chiffon Cake

Sifted cake flour	2 1/4 cups	550 mL
Granulated sugar	1 1/2 cups	375 mL
Baking powder	1 tbsp.	15 mL
Salt	1 tsp.	5 mL
Egg whites (large), room temperature	1 cup	250 mL
Cream of tartar	1/2 tsp.	2 mL
Egg yolks (large)	5	5
Orange juice	3/4 cup	175 mL
Cooking oil	1/2 cup	125 mL
Grated orange zest (see Tip, page 56)	1 tbsp.	15 mL
Vanilla extract	1 tsp.	5 mL

Measure first 4 ingredients into sieve over large bowl. Sift into bowl. Make a well in centre. Set aside.

Beat egg whites and cream of tartar in separate large bowl until stiff peaks form.

Add remaining 5 ingredients to well in flour mixture. Beat until smooth. Fold about 1/4 of egg white mixture into orange mixture. Add remaining egg white mixture in 2 additions, gently folding after each addition until no white streaks remain. Spread in ungreased 10 inch (25 cm) angel food tube pan. Bake in 325°F (160°C) oven for 60 to 70 minutes until wooden pick inserted in centre of cake comes out clean. Invert cake in pan onto glass bottle for 2 to 3 hours until cooled completely (see Tip). Turn upright. Run knife around inside edge of pan to loosen cake. Remove bottom of pan with cake. Run knife around tube and bottom of pan to loosen. Invert cake onto large serving plate. Cuts into 16 wedges.

1 wedge: 218 Calories; 8.6 g Total Fat (4.7 g Mono, 2.3 g Poly, 1.0 g Sat); 59 mg Cholesterol; 32 g Carbohydrate; trace Fibre; 4 g Protein; 220 mg Sodium

Pictured at right.

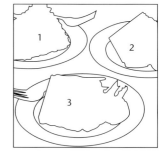

1. Lemon Coconut Angel, page 39
2. Orange Chiffon Cake, above
3. Burnt Sugar Angel Food, page 38

Filled with delicious tropical flavours, this delightful dessert gives you a chance to work with passion fruit. Macadamia nuts give this treat extra flavour and richness.

about passion fruit

Shrivelled, wrinkly—and pretty delicious! While most fruits are eaten when their skins are firm and smooth, a smooth-skinned passion fruit is nowhere near ripe and should be allowed to sit at room temperature until it is properly wrinkled. When your passion fruit is fully ripe, simply slice it open and spoon out the soft pulp, which can then be eaten plain or used in desserts. Ripe passion fruits will keep in the fridge for up to a week.

Mango Torte

MERINGUE

Egg whites (large), room temperature	4	4
Cream of tartar	1/2 tsp.	2 mL
Granulated sugar	1 cup	250 mL
Macadamia nuts, toasted (see Tip, page 48), finely chopped	2/3 cup	150 mL

FILLING

Can of sliced mango in syrup, drained	14 oz.	398 mL
Whipping cream	1 1/2 cups	375 mL
Icing (confectioner's) sugar	1/2 cup	125 mL

TOPPING

Passion fruit pulp (about 4 – 6 passion fruits)	1/2 cup	125 mL
Granulated sugar	1/3 cup	75 mL
Can of sliced mango in syrup, drained and cut into thin slices	14 oz.	398 mL

Meringue: Line 2 baking sheets with parchment (not waxed) paper. Trace two 7 inch (18 cm) circles about 2 inches (5 cm) apart on first paper, and one 7 inch (18 cm) circle on second paper. Turn papers over. Beat egg whites and cream of tartar in large bowl until soft peaks form. Add sugar, 1 tbsp. (15 mL) at a time, beating constantly until sugar is dissolved.

Fold in macadamia nuts. Spoon onto circles. Spread evenly to edge of each circle. Bake in 325°F (160°C) oven for about 50 minutes until golden and dry. Let stand on baking sheets until cool.

Filling: Put mango into blender or food processor. Process until smooth.

Beat whipping cream in medium bowl until soft peaks form. Beat in icing sugar until well combined. Fold in processed mango. Place 1 meringue on serving plate. Spread 1/3 of filling on top. Place second meringue over filling. Spread half of remaining filling over top. Place third meringue over filling. Spread remaining filling on top. Chill, covered, for at least 8 hours or overnight.

(continued on next page)

Topping: Combine passion fruit pulp and sugar in small frying pan. Heat and stir on medium for about 5 minutes until slightly thickened. Cool. Strain, reserving 2 tbsp. (30 mL) seeds. Discard remaining seeds. Stir reserved seeds into strained passion fruit mixture.

Arrange mango slices over filling. Drizzle passion fruit mixture over top. Serve immediately. Cuts into 8 wedges.

1 wedge: 479 Calories; 24.2 g Total Fat (11.2 g Mono, 0.8 g Poly, 11.1 g Sat); 57 mg Cholesterol; 67 g Carbohydrate; 3 g Fibre; 4 g Protein; 51 mg Sodium

Pictured on page 45.

Pineapple Coconut Meringues

Can of pineapple slices, drained	14 oz.	398 mL
Sliced natural almonds	1/4 cup	60 mL
Egg whites (large), room temperature	2	2
Vanilla extract	1/2 tsp.	2 mL
Granulated sugar	2 tbsp.	30 mL
Medium unsweetened coconut	1/3 cup	75 mL
Sliced natural almonds	1/4 cup	60 mL
Medium unsweetened coconut	3 tbsp.	50 mL

A sweet treat that mirrors the flavours of the islands. These fluffy meringues are made even more tempting with the addition of coconut.

Arrange 4 stacks of 2 pineapple slices in greased 9 inch (22 cm) pie plate. Sprinkle first amount of almonds over top. Set aside.

Beat egg whites in medium bowl until soft peaks form. Add vanilla. Add sugar, 1 tbsp. (15 mL) at a time, beating constantly until stiff peaks form and sugar is dissolved.

Fold first amount of coconut and second amount of almonds into egg white mixture. Spoon onto pineapple.

Sprinkle with second amount of coconut. Bake in 400°F (205°C) oven for about 10 minutes until meringue is golden. Serves 4.

1 serving: 276 Calories; 15.2 g Total Fat (6.0 g Mono, 2.2 g Poly, 6.2 g Sat); 0 mg Cholesterol; 32 g Carbohydrate; 4 g Fibre; 6 g Protein; 44 mg Sodium

Pictured on page 45.

"Orange" you tempted to try this citrusy, light dessert? We know you are and you'll be glad you did. It's totally refreshing.

Orange Swirls

MERINGUES		
Egg whites (large), room temperature	3	3
Cream of tartar	1/4 tsp.	1 mL
Granulated sugar	1/2 cup	125 mL
Icing (confectioner's) sugar, sifted	1/2 cup	125 mL
FILLING		
Egg yolks (large)	3	3
Orange juice	1/4 cup	60 mL
Frozen concentrated orange juice	3 tbsp.	50 mL
Granulated sugar	3 tbsp.	50 mL
Grated orange zest	2 tsp.	10 mL
Whipping cream (or 1 envelope of dessert topping, prepared)	1 cup	250 mL

Orange segments, for garnish

Meringues: Line bottom of 11 x 17 inch (28 x 43 cm) baking sheet with parchment (not waxed) paper. Trace six 3 inch (7.5 cm) circles about 2 inches (5 cm) apart on paper. Turn paper over. Beat egg whites and cream of tartar in large bowl until soft peaks form. Add granulated sugar, 1 tbsp. (15 mL) at a time, beating constantly until stiff peaks form and sugar is dissolved.

Fold icing sugar into egg white mixture. Spoon into piping bag fitted with small open star tip. Pipe onto circles, filling each circle completely. Pipe meringue around edge of each circle twice to make sides. Bake in 200°F (95°C) oven for about 1 hour until dry. Turn oven off. Let stand in oven until cool.

Filling: Combine first 4 ingredients in top of double boiler or heatproof bowl set over simmering water. Cook, stirring constantly with whisk, until thickened. Remove from heat.

Add orange zest. Stir. Cover with plastic wrap directly on surface to prevent skin from forming. Chill until cooled completely.

Beat whipping cream until soft peaks form. Fold into orange mixture until no white streaks remain. Spoon into meringues. Chill for 1 hour.

Garnish with orange segments. Serves 6.

1 serving: 311 Calories; 16.5 g Total Fat (5.1 g Mono, 0.9 g Poly, 9.4 g Sat); 146 mg Cholesterol; 38 g Carbohydrate; trace Fibre; 4 g Protein; 46 mg Sodium

Pictured at right.

1. Mango Torte, page 42
2. Orange Swirls, page 44
3. Pineapple Coconut Meringues, page 43

Chocolate Charlotte Russe

Envelopes of unflavoured gelatin (1/4 oz., 7 g, each)	2	2
Milk	2 1/2 cups	625 mL
Granulated sugar	2/3 cup	150 mL
Cocoa, sifted if lumpy	1/2 cup	125 mL
Salt	1/4 tsp.	1 mL
Egg yolks (large)	3	3
Milk	2 tbsp.	30 mL
Vanilla extract	1 tsp.	5 mL
Egg whites (large), room temperature (see Tip, page 83)	3	3
Granulated sugar	1/3 cup	75 mL
Frozen whipped topping, thawed (or 1 envelope of dessert topping, prepared)	2 cups	500 mL
Giant ladyfingers	30	30

Sprinkle gelatin over first amount of milk in medium saucepan. Let stand for 1 minute. Heat and stir on low until gelatin is dissolved. Bring to a boil.

Combine next 3 ingredients in small bowl.

Add next 3 ingredients. Stir. Add to boiling gelatin mixture, stirring constantly, until just thickened. Set saucepan in bowl of ice water. Let stand, stirring and scraping down sides often, until mixture will mound slightly. The mixture will thicken quickly as it cools.

Beat egg whites in medium bowl until soft peaks form. Add second amount of sugar, 1 tbsp. (15 mL) at a time, beating constantly until stiff peaks form and sugar is dissolved. Fold into gelatin mixture.

Fold in whipped topping.

Cut 1 inch (2.5 cm) piece off 1 end of each ladyfinger. Set pieces aside. Stand ladyfingers rounded-side out, cut-side down around inside edge of greased 10 inch (25 cm) springform pan. Lay remaining ladyfingers and reserved pieces in single layer in bottom of pan, breaking to fit as necessary. Spoon gelatin mixture into pan, keeping ladyfingers upright. Chill until firm. Cuts into 10 wedges.

(continued on next page)

*1 wedge: 302 Calories; 8.9 g Total Fat (2.5 g Mono, 0.8 g Poly, 5.5 g Sat); 181 mg Cholesterol;
49 g Carbohydrate; 2 g Fibre; 9 g Protein; 172 mg Sodium*

Pictured below.

Make simple pound cake and vanilla ice cream spectacular. When you serve them with liqueur-soaked berries, you won't believe the compliments you'll get.

When toasting nuts, seeds or coconut, cooking times will vary for each type of nut—so never toast them together. For small amounts, place ingredient in an ungreased shallow frying pan. Heat on medium for 3 to 5 minutes, stirring often, until golden. For larger amounts, spread ingredient evenly in an ungreased shallow pan. Bake in a 350°F (175°C) oven for 5 to 10 minutes, stirring or shaking often, until golden.

Swirl Ice Cream With Grilled Cake And Berries

Vanilla ice cream, softened	2 cups	500 mL
Sliced almonds, toasted (see Tip)	1/3 cup	75 mL
Chocolate sauce	1/2 cup	125 mL
Orange juice	1/2 cup	125 mL
Butter (or hard margarine), melted	1/4 cup	60 mL
Brown sugar, packed	2 tbsp.	30 mL
Grated orange zest	1 tsp.	5 mL
Ground ginger	3/4 tsp.	4 mL
Frozen pound cake, thawed	10 1/2 oz.	298 g
Frozen mixed berries, thawed, with juice	3 cups	750 mL
Icing (confectioner's) sugar	1/4 cup	60 mL
Orange liqueur	3 tbsp.	50 mL

Put ice cream into medium bowl. Add almonds. Stir. Swirl chocolate sauce through ice cream. Freeze, covered, for 2 to 3 hours until firm.

Combine next 5 ingredients in small bowl.

Preheat gas barbecue to medium. Cut off top of cake to make flat. Cut cake crosswise into 6 slices. Cut slices in half diagonally. Brush cake pieces liberally with orange juice mixture. Cook on well greased grill for about 3 minutes per side until browned.

Combine remaining 3 ingredients in medium bowl. Scoop ice cream mixture onto 6 individual serving plates. Arrange 2 cake pieces on each plate. Spoon berry mixture over top. Serves 6.

1 serving: 664 Calories; 35.0 g Total Fat (8.4 g Mono, 2.0 g Poly, 16.6 g Sat); 137 mg Cholesterol; 77 g Carbohydrate; 4 g Fibre; 9 g Protein; 293 mg Sodium

Pictured at right.

A light bit of fluff it is! A fresh taste after a heavier meal.

Mango Rum Fluff

Envelope of unflavoured gelatin (about 1 tbsp., 15 mL)	1/4 oz.	7 g
Cold water	1/4 cup	60 mL
Granulated sugar	1/2 cup	125 mL
Lemon juice	1 tbsp.	15 mL
Salt, just a pinch		
Can of sliced mango in syrup, drained, puréed	14 oz.	398 mL
Amber (golden) rum (or 1/2 tsp., 2 mL, rum extract)	1 tbsp.	15 mL
Almond extract	1/4 tsp.	1 mL
Whipping cream	1 cup	250 mL
Amber (golden) rum (or 1/4 tsp., 1 mL, rum extract)	1 1/2 tsp.	7 mL
Slivered almonds, toasted (see Tip, page 48)	1 tbsp.	15 mL

Sprinkle gelatin over cold water in small saucepan. Let stand for 1 minute. Heat and stir on low until gelatin is dissolved.

Add next 3 ingredients. Stir until sugar is dissolved. Remove from heat.

Add next 3 ingredients. Mix well. Transfer to large serving bowl. Chill for about 1 hour, stirring occasionally, until mixture is starting to thicken.

Beat whipping cream in small bowl until soft peaks form. Transfer 1/2 cup (125 mL) to small dish. Fold remaining whipped cream into mango mixture. Chill.

Fold second amount of rum into reserved whipped cream. Pipe over mango mixture around inside edge of serving bowl. Sprinkle with almonds. Serves 6.

1 serving: 266 Calories; 14.6 g Total Fat (4.5 g Mono, 0.7 g Poly, 8.7 g Sat); 51 mg Cholesterol; 33 g Carbohydrate; 1 g Fibre; 2 g Protein; 20 mg Sodium

Pictured on page 53.

Raspberry Swirl

Try this pretty, summertime-fresh dessert. Lovely swirls of creamy white and raspberry red are sure to impress.

SHORTBREAD CRUST

All-purpose flour	1 cup	250 mL
Granulated sugar	2 tbsp.	30 mL
Cold butter (or hard margarine), cut up	1/2 cup	125 mL

FILLING

Box of raspberry jelly powder (gelatin)	3 oz.	85 g
Boiling water	3/4 cup	175 mL
Container of frozen raspberries in syrup (15 oz., 425 g), partially thawed	1/2	1/2
Milk	1/2 cup	125 mL
Large marshmallows	16	16
Whipped cream (or 1 envelope of dessert topping, prepared)	2 cups	500 mL

Shortbread Crust: Combine flour and sugar in medium bowl. Cut in butter until mixture resembles coarse crumbs. Press firmly in ungreased 9 × 9 inch (22 × 22 cm) pan. Bake in 350°F (175°C) oven for about 15 minutes until golden. Cool.

Filling: Stir jelly powder into boiling water in medium heatproof bowl until dissolved. Stir in berries. Chill until mixture is syrup consistency.

Heat milk in large heavy saucepan on medium-low until hot, but not boiling. Add marshmallows. Heat and stir until melted. Cool, stirring occasionally.

Fold marshmallow mixture into whipped cream. Fold into raspberry mixture leaving some white streaks. Spread evenly over crust. Chill. Cuts into 9 pieces.

1 piece: 308 Calories; 13.8 g Total Fat (2.7 g Mono, 0.4 g Poly, 10.0 g Sat); 28 mg Cholesterol; 45 g Carbohydrate; 1 g Fibre; 3 g Protein; 134 mg Sodium

Pictured on page 53.

This has to be one of the quickest and easiest desserts ever—and so delightfully refreshing! You'll be able to whip it up in no time.

Lemon Chiffon

Envelope of lemon pie filling (not instant), enough for 1 pie	1	1
Egg yolks (large)	2	2
Egg whites (large), room temperature (see Tip, page 83)	2	2

Prepare pie filling according to package directions, using 2 egg yolks. Remove from heat.

Beat egg whites in small bowl until stiff peaks form. Fold into hot pie filling. Pour into 6 individual serving bowls. Chill until firm. Serves 6.

1 serving: 392 Calories; 7.4 g Total Fat (3.2 g Mono, 1.6 g Poly, 1.8 g Sat); 146 mg Cholesterol; 77 g Carbohydrate; 1 g Fibre; 6 g Protein; 108 mg Sodium

Pictured on page 53.

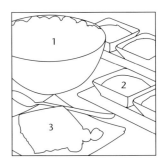

1. Mango Rum Fluff, page 50
2. Lemon Chiffon, above
3. Raspberry Swirl, page 51

Imagine a lemon meringue pie with the filling and meringue all folded together—the result is a darling fluffy pie with tart lemon flavour. Garnish with a little whipped cream and slices of fresh lemon for a fancier presentation.

Lemon Mousse Pie

Eggs yolks (large)	5	5
Granulated sugar	3/4 cup	175 mL
Lemon juice	6 tbsp.	100 mL
Grated lemon zest	1 tsp.	5 mL
Egg whites (large), room temperature	5	5
Baked 9 inch (22 cm) pie shell (see Tip, page 60)		

Beat egg yolks and sugar in top of double boiler or heatproof bowl set over simmering water until slightly thickened.

Stir in lemon juice and lemon zest. Cook for about 10 minutes, stirring constantly, until thickened. Remove top of double boiler or bowl to wire rack. Let stand for about 10 minutes until cool.

Using clean beaters, beat egg whites in large bowl until stiff peaks form. Fold into lemon mixture until no white streaks remain.

Spoon into pie shell. Bake in 350°F (175°C) oven for about 15 minutes until golden. Cool. Cuts into 8 wedges.

1 wedge: 200 Calories; 8.3 g Total Fat (3.8 g Mono, 1.1 g Poly, 2.6 g Sat); 119 mg Cholesterol; 27 g Carbohydrate; trace Fibre; 5 g Protein; 140 mg Sodium

Pictured on page 57.

This beautiful strawberry-filled roll is perfect for a shower, a farewell party or any occasion when you want to impress your guests.

Angel Roll

Box of angel food cake mix	15 oz.	430 g
Icing (confectioner's) sugar, approximately	2 tbsp.	30 mL
FILLING		
Reserved syrup from strawberries		
Cornstarch	2 tbsp.	30 mL
Containers of frozen strawberries in light syrup (15 oz., 425 g, each), thawed, drained and syrup reserved	2	2
Envelopes of dessert topping (prepared), or 4 cups (1 L) whipped cream	2	2

(continued on next page)

Line bottom of 2 ungreased 11 × 17 inch (28 × 43 cm) baking sheets with sides with parchment (or waxed) paper. Prepare cake mix according to package directions. Pour into prepared pans. Spread evenly. Bake in 375°F (190°C) oven for 8 to 10 minutes until golden. Let stand in pans on wire rack for 5 minutes. Run knife around inside edges of pans to loosen cakes. Spread 2 large tea towels on work surface. Cover with sheets of waxed paper.

Sift icing sugar onto waxed paper. Invert cakes onto icing sugar. Carefully peel off and discard parchment paper from bottoms of cakes. Roll up cakes from short ends, with towel and waxed paper. Let stand until cool.

Filling: Stir reserved strawberry syrup into cornstarch in medium saucepan. Heat and stir on medium until boiling and thickened. Cool completely. Add strawberries. Stir. Unroll cakes. Spread half of strawberry mixture evenly over each cake, leaving 1/2 inch (12 mm) border.

Spread half of whipped topping over strawberry mixture on each cake. Roll up gently, using waxed paper as a guide. Place rolls, seam-side down, on serving plate. Each roll cuts into 10 slices, for a total of 20 slices.

1 slice: 123 Calories; 3.3 g Total Fat (trace Mono, trace Poly, 3.2 g Sat); 0 mg Cholesterol; 23 g Carbohydrate; trace Fibre; 2 g Protein; 117 mg Sodium

Pictured below.　　　　　　　　　　　　　　　　　　　Angel Roll, page 54

Upside-Down Lemon Pie

MERINGUE CRUST

Egg whites (large), room temperature	3	3
Cream of tartar	1/4 tsp.	1 mL
Salt	1/8 tsp.	0.5 mL
Granulated sugar	3/4 cup	175 mL
Vanilla wafer crumbs	1/2 cup	125 mL
Vanilla extract	1 tsp.	5 mL
Sliced almonds	1/3 cup	75 mL

FILLING

Granulated sugar	1 cup	250 mL
Cornstarch	1/3 cup	75 mL
Egg yolks (large), fork-beaten	3	3
Hot water	2 cups	500 mL
Drops of yellow food colouring (optional)	2	2
Lemon juice	1/3 cup	75 mL
Butter (or hard margarine)	1 tbsp.	15 mL
Grated lemon zest (see Tip)	1 tbsp.	15 mL
Salt	1/4 tsp.	1 mL

TOPPING

Whipping cream (optional)	3/4 cup	175 mL
Vanilla wafer crumbs	2 tbsp.	30 mL

Meringue Crust: Beat first 3 ingredients in medium bowl until soft peaks form. Add sugar, 1 tbsp. (15 mL) at a time, beating constantly until stiff peaks form and sugar is dissolved.

Fold in wafer crumbs and vanilla. Spread in bottom and sides of greased 9 inch (22 cm) pie plate.

Sprinkle with almonds. Bake in 325°F (160°C) oven for about 30 minutes until dry. Let stand on wire rack until cooled completely.

Filling: Combine sugar and cornstarch in medium saucepan. Add next 3 ingredients. Heat and stir on medium until boiling and thickened. Remove from heat.

Add next 4 ingredients. Stir well. Cool. Spread evenly in meringue crust.

(continued on next page)

Topping: Beat whipping cream in small bowl until soft peaks form. Spread evenly over filling. Sprinkle with wafer crumbs. Chill for 30 minutes. Cuts into 8 wedges.

1 wedge: *291 Calories; 7.3 g Total Fat (3.5 g Mono, 1.3 g Poly, 2.0 g Sat); 78 mg Cholesterol;*
54 g Carbohydrate; 1 g Fibre; 4 g Protein; 165 mg Sodium

Pictured below.

1. Lime Meringue Pie, page 58
2. Lemon Mousse Pie, page 54
3. Upside-Down Lemon Pie, page 56

Citrus fruits are definitely not all the same, so if you're expecting this Lime Meringue Pie to taste like its lemon counterpart, you need to raise your expectations. It's a whole new flavour sensation.

about blind baking

Put that blindfold away! Blind baking is simply an English term for baking a pie crust before the filling is added. The pastry is usually pricked with a fork and lined with foil or parchment paper, then filled with some kind of weight to keep it from puffing up. You can buy fancy ceramic pie weights, but dried beans work just as well. We don't recommend eating the beans after they've been baked, but you can use them again the next time you want to make a pie.

Lime Meringue Pie

CRUST

All-purpose flour	1 cup	250 mL
Cold butter (or hard margarine), cut up	1/2 cup	125 mL
Egg yolks (large)	2	2
Cold water, approximately	1 tbsp.	15 mL

FILLING

Granulated sugar	1 1/2 cups	375 mL
Cornstarch	1/2 cup	125 mL
Lime juice	1/2 cup	125 mL
Water	1/2 cup	125 mL
Egg yolks (large)	3	3
Butter (or hard margarine), softened	2 tbsp.	30 mL
Boiling water	1 1/2 cups	375 mL
Grated lime zest	1 tsp.	5 mL
Drops of green food colouring (optional)	2	2

MERINGUE

Egg whites (large), room temperature	5	5
Berry sugar	1 1/4 cups	300 mL

Crust: Measure flour into medium bowl. Cut in butter until mixture resembles coarse crumbs. Mix in egg yolks and enough cold water to make smooth dough. Wrap with plastic wrap. Chill for 15 minutes. Roll out pastry on lightly floured surface to fit 9 inch (22 cm) pie plate. Trim, leaving 1/2 inch (12 mm) overhang. Roll under and crimp decorative edge. Cover pastry with parchment paper, bringing paper up over crimped edge. Fill halfway up side with dried beans. Bake on bottom rack in 400°F (205°C) oven for 10 minutes. Carefully remove paper and beans, reserving beans for next time you bake pastry. Bake for 5 to 7 minutes until browned. Let stand on wire rack until cool.

Filling: Whisk first 4 ingredients in medium saucepan until smooth. Add egg yolks and butter. Stir well.

Slowly add boiling water, stirring constantly. Heat and stir on medium until boiling and thickened. Reduce heat to medium-low. Simmer, uncovered, for 1 minute. Remove from heat. Add lime zest and food colouring. Mix well. Spread evenly in pie shell.

(continued on next page)

Meringue: Beat egg whites in medium bowl until soft peaks form. Add berry sugar, 1/4 cup (60 mL) at a time, beating constantly until stiff peaks form and sugar is dissolved. Spoon or pipe meringue over filling. Bake in 350°F (175°C) oven for 10 to 15 minutes until golden. Cool. Cuts into 8 wedges.

1 wedge: 513 Calories; 17.4 g Total Fat (5.0 g Mono, 1.0 g Poly, 10.0 g Sat); 156 mg Cholesterol; 86 g Carbohydrate; trace Fibre; 6 g Protein; 140 mg Sodium

Pictured on page 57.

Orange Soufflé Clouds

Granulated sugar	2 tbsp.	30 mL
Skim milk	1 cup	250 mL
Granulated sugar	3 tbsp.	50 mL
Cornstarch	2 tbsp.	30 mL
Egg yolk (large), fork-beaten	1	1
Orange juice	1/3 cup	75 mL
Grated orange zest (see Tip, page 56)	1 tbsp.	15 mL
Egg whites (large), room temperature	5	5
Cream of tartar	1/2 tsp.	2 mL
Granulated sugar	3 tbsp.	50 mL

Sprinkle first amount of sugar into greased 6 oz. (170 mL) ramekin. Tilt ramekin to coat bottom and sides with sugar. Gently tap excess sugar into another greased ramekin. Repeat 5 more times to prepare a total of 6 sugar-coated ramekins. Discard excess sugar from last ramekin once coated. Place ramekins on baking sheet with sides. Set aside.

Combine next 3 ingredients in small saucepan. Heat and stir on medium for about 5 minutes until boiling and thickened.

Combine next 3 ingredients in small cup. Add to milk mixture, stirring constantly with whisk for about 1 minute until thick. Transfer to medium bowl.

Beat egg whites and cream of tartar in large bowl until soft peaks form. Add third amount of sugar, 1 tbsp. (15 mL) at a time, beating constantly until stiff peaks form and sugar is dissolved. Fold about 1/3 of egg white mixture into hot milk mixture until almost combined. Fold milk mixture into remaining egg whites until no white streaks remain. Spoon into ramekins. Smooth tops. Bake in 400°F (205°C) oven for about 12 minutes, without opening oven door, until very puffed and tops are golden. Serve immediately. Serves 6.

1 serving: 115 Calories; 1.0 g Total Fat (0.4 g Mono, 0.1 g Poly, 0.3 g Sat); 32 mg Cholesterol; 22 g Carbohydrate; trace Fibre; 5 g Protein; 68 mg Sodium

These individual soufflés will have you feeling lighter than air.

about soufflés

Far from being as persnickety as people believe, soufflés are actually pretty easy to make— as long as you keep a few things in mind. Air trapped inside the soufflé causes it to puff up while baking, creating that light, delicate texture. However, the air starts to escape as soon as the soufflé comes in contact with cold air, which is why you should never open the oven door while the soufflé is baking, and why you should serve it as quickly as possible after removing it from the oven.

A "sweet-tart" of a pie! Golden meringue on a bright raspberry-red filling. The perfect combination of sweetness and tang.

tip

Not sure how to get a baked pie shell? You can either make your own pastry and line a pie plate or purchase ready-made pie shells from the grocery store. Cover the pastry with parchment paper, bringing paper up over the edge. Fill halfway with dried beans. Bake on the bottom rack in 375°F (190°C) oven for 15 minutes. Carefully remove paper and beans. You can save the beans for the next time you bake pastry. Bake for another 20 minutes until lightly browned. Be sure to let the pastry cool before adding your filling. If you're not crazy about the bean idea, you can also insert another pie plate on top of your crust, turn both plates upside down and bake. Also, if you're using a store-bought 9 inch (22 cm), deep-dish crust, you can just pop it straight in the oven to bake.

Raspberry Meringue Pie

FILLING

Container of frozen raspberries in syrup, thawed	15 oz.	425 g
Granulated sugar	1 cup	250 mL
Cornstarch	1/2 cup	125 mL
Lemon juice	1/2 cup	125 mL
Egg yolks (large), fork-beaten	3	3
Butter (or hard margarine), cut up	1/3 cup	75 mL
Grated lemon zest (see Tip, page 56)	1 tbsp.	15 mL
Baked 9 inch (22 cm) pie shell (see Tip)		

MERINGUE

Egg whites (large), room temperature	3	3
Granulated sugar	1/2 cup	125 mL

Filling: Put raspberries with syrup into blender or food processor. Process until smooth. Strain through sieve into small bowl. Discard seeds.

Combine sugar and cornstarch in medium saucepan. Stir in lemon juice and raspberry mixture until smooth. Heat and stir on medium for about 5 minutes until boiling and thickened. Reduce heat to medium-low.

Add next 3 ingredients, stirring constantly. Heat and stir for about 1 minute until boiling and butter is melted. Remove from heat.

Pour raspberry mixture into pie shell. Spread evenly.

Meringue: Beat egg whites in medium bowl until soft peaks form. Add sugar, 1 tbsp. (15 mL) at a time, beating constantly until stiff peaks form and sugar is dissolved. Spoon over filling. Spread evenly to edge of pastry. Swirl meringue to create decorative peaks. Bake in 350°F (175°C) oven for 10 to 12 minutes until golden. Cool. Cuts into 8 wedges.

1 wedge: 436 Calories; 14.6 g Total Fat (5.2 g Mono, 1.2 g Poly, 7.0 g Sat); 91 mg Cholesterol; 74 g Carbohydrate; 2 g Fibre; 4 g Protein; 192 mg Sodium

Pictured at right.

Maraschino cherries give this glorious pie its pink colour. A lush, juicy treat with an excellent shortbread crust.

Imagine an ice cream sundae or black forest cake without those bright red maraschino cherries on top. Not quite the same, is it? Maraschino cherries originally got their name from a liqueur made from the Marasca cherry, in which they were once preserved. Nowadays, they're more commonly saturated in a red-coloured sugar syrup.

Pineapple Glory Pie

SHORTBREAD CRUST		
All-purpose flour	1 1/2 cups	375 mL
Granulated sugar	2 tbsp.	30 mL
Butter (or hard margarine)	3/4 cup	175 mL
FILLING		
Can of crushed pineapple (with juice)	19 oz.	540 mL
Granulated sugar	2/3 cup	150 mL
Cornstarch	3 tbsp.	50 mL
Lemon juice	1 tsp.	5 mL
Chopped maraschino cherries	1/3 cup	75 mL
Maraschino cherry juice	3 tbsp.	50 mL
Almond extract	1 tsp.	5 mL
MERINGUE		
Egg whites (large), room temperature	3	3
Cream of tartar	1/4 tsp.	1 mL
Granulated sugar	1/4 cup	60 mL
Vanilla extract	1 tsp.	5 mL
Medium unsweetened coconut	2 tbsp.	30 mL

Shortbread Crust: Combine flour and sugar in medium bowl. Cut in butter until mixture resembles coarse crumbs. Press firmly in bottom and up side of 9 inch (22 cm) pie plate. Bake in 350°F (175°C) oven for about 15 minutes until golden. Cool.

Filling: Stir first 4 ingredients in small saucepan until cornstarch is dissolved. Heat and stir on medium until boiling and thickened. Remove from heat.

Stir in next 3 ingredients. Pour into crust.

Meringue: Beat egg whites and cream of tartar until soft peaks form. Add sugar, 1 tbsp. (15 mL) at a time, beating constantly until stiff peaks form and sugar is dissolved. Add vanilla. Stir. Spoon over filling. Spread evenly to edge of pastry.

Sprinkle with coconut. Bake in 350°F (175°C) oven for 10 to 12 minutes until golden. Cool. Cuts into 8 wedges.

1 wedge: 409 Calories; 17.8 g Total Fat (4.5 g Mono, 0.7 g Poly, 11.5 g Sat); 45 mg Cholesterol; 59 g Carbohydrate; 2 g Fibre; 4 g Protein; 149 mg Sodium

Pictured on page 61.

Banana Cream Pie

Box of instant vanilla pudding powder (6-serving size)	1	1
Milk	1 cup	250 mL
Frozen whipped topping, thawed	1 cup	250 mL
Medium bananas, sliced	2	2
Chocolate (or graham cracker) crumb crust (9 inch, 22 cm, diameter)	1	1
Frozen whipped topping, thawed	1 cup	250 mL
Banana chips, for garnish		

The perfect banana cream pie. Creamy and rich, yet not overly sweet. Simple and delicious.

Beat pudding powder and milk in medium bowl until smooth.

Fold in first amount of whipped topping and banana. Spread evenly in crumb crust.

Spread second amount of whipped topping evenly over pudding mixture.

Garnish with banana chips. Cuts into 8 wedges.

1 wedge: 285 Calories; 11.9 g Total Fat (3.6 g Mono, 2.1 g Poly, 5.8 g Sat); 2 mg Cholesterol; 44 g Carbohydrate; 1 g Fibre; 3 g Protein; 381 mg Sodium

Pictured on page 61.

Family and friends will go nuts for these sweet squares. They'll know you're not green when it comes to making great desserts!

Pistachio Dessert

NUTTY SHORTBREAD CRUST

All-purpose flour	1 cup	250 mL
Finely chopped pecans	1/2 cup	125 mL
Butter (or hard margarine), softened	1/2 cup	125 mL

FILLING

Block of cream cheese, softened	8 oz.	250 g
Icing (confectioner's) sugar	1 cup	250 mL
Box of instant pistachio pudding powder (6-serving size)	1	1
Milk	2 cups	500 mL

TOPPING

Whipping cream (or 1 envelope of dessert topping, prepared)	1 cup	250 mL
Slivered almonds	3 tbsp.	50 mL

Nutty Shortbread Crust: Combine flour and pecans in medium bowl. Cut in butter until mixture resembles coarse crumbs. Press firmly in ungreased 9 x 13 inch (22 x 33 cm) pan. Bake in 350°F (175°C) oven for about 15 minutes until golden. Cool.

Filling: Beat cream cheese in small bowl until smooth. Add icing sugar. Mix well. Spread evenly over crust.

Using same beaters, beat pudding powder and milk in separate small bowl until thickened. Spread evenly over cream cheese mixture. Chill until set.

Topping: Beat whipping cream in medium bowl until soft peaks form. Spread evenly over pudding mixture. Sprinkle with almonds. Cuts into 15 pieces.

1 piece: 324 Calories; 21.3 g Total Fat (7.0 g Mono, 1.7 g Poly, 11.1 g Sat); 54 mg Cholesterol; 30 g Carbohydrate; 1 g Fibre; 4 g Protein; 314 mg Sodium

Pictured on page 65.

A peachy-keen combination of cream cheese and peaches gives this goodie a tantalizing taste.

Peaches And Cream

CRUST

Butter (or hard margarine)	1/2 cup	125 mL
Graham cracker crumbs	2 cups	500 mL
Brown sugar, packed	1/3 cup	75 mL

(continued on next page)

FILLING

Cans of sliced peaches in juice (14 oz., 398 mL, each), drained and juice reserved	2	2
Reserved juice from peaches (see Tip)	2 cups	500 mL
Cornstarch	1/4 cup	60 mL
Granulated sugar	1/4 cup	60 mL
Whipping cream (or 2 envelopes of dessert topping, prepared)	2 cups	500 mL
Block of cream cheese, softened	8 oz.	250 g
Granulated sugar	1 cup	250 mL

Crust: Melt butter in small saucepan on medium. Remove from heat. Add graham crumbs and brown sugar. Stir well. Reserve 1/2 cup (125 mL) for topping. Press remaining crumb mixture firmly into ungreased 9 × 13 (22 × 33 cm) pan. Bake in 350°F (175°C) oven for 10 minutes. Cool.

Filling: Combine first 4 ingredients in small saucepan. Heat and stir on medium until boiling and thickened. Cool.

Beat whipping cream in medium bowl until soft peaks form. Using same beaters, beat cream cheese and sugar in separate medium bowl until light and fluffy. Fold whipped cream into cream cheese mixture. Spread half of cream cheese mixture evenly over crust. Spoon peach mixture over cream cheese mixture. Spread remaining cream cheese mixture evenly over top. Sprinkle with reserved crumb mixture. Chill until firm. Cuts into 15 pieces.

1 piece: 386 Calories; 23.6 g Total Fat (6.8 g Mono, 1.3 g Poly, 14.2 g Sat); 73 mg Cholesterol; 43 g Carbohydrate; 1 g Fibre; 3 g Protein; 172 mg Sodium

Pictured on page 67.

tip

Not enough peach juice in your cans of peaches? Simply top up with water or store-bought peach nectar to make 2 cups (500 mL).

Left: Chilled Chocolate Dessert page 68
Right: Pistachio Dessert, page 64

Even though it seems there are lots of ingredients, trust us, this vibrantly-coloured treat isn't broken. It's super simple to make.

Broken Glass

CRUST

Butter (or hard margarine)	1/2 cup	125 mL
Graham cracker crumbs	2 cups	500 mL
Brown sugar, packed	1/4 cup	60 mL

FILLING

Box of raspberry jelly powder (gelatin)	3 oz.	85 g
Boiling water	1 1/2 cups	375 mL
Box of lime jelly powder (gelatin)	3 oz.	85 g
Boiling water	1 1/2 cups	375 mL
Box of lemon jelly powder (gelatin)	3 oz.	85 g
Boiling water	1 1/2 cups	375 mL
Envelope of unflavoured gelatin (about 1 tbsp., 15 mL)	1/4 oz.	7 g
Cold water	1/4 cup	60 mL
Pineapple juice	1 cup	250 mL
Whipping cream (or 2 envelopes of dessert topping, prepared), see Note	2 cups	500 mL
Granulated sugar	2 tbsp.	30 mL
Vanilla extract	1 tsp.	5 mL

Crust: Melt butter in small saucepan on medium. Remove from heat. Add graham crumbs and brown sugar. Stir well. Press firmly in ungreased 9 x 13 (22 x 33 cm) pan. Bake in 350°F (175°C) oven for 10 minutes. Cool.

Filling: Stir raspberry jelly powder into boiling water in small heatproof bowl until dissolved. Pour into shallow pan so gelatin will be about 1/4 inch (6 mm) thick. Chill until set.

Stir lime jelly powder into boiling water in separate small heatproof bowl until dissolved. Pour into separate shallow pan so gelatin will be about 1/4 inch (6 mm) thick. Chill until set.

Stir lemon jelly powder into boiling water in separate small heatproof bowl until dissolved. Pour into separate shallow pan so gelatin will be about 1/4 inch (6 mm) thick. Chill until set.

Sprinkle unflavoured gelatin over cold water in small saucepan. Let stand for 1 minute. Add pineapple juice. Heat and stir on low until gelatin is dissolved. Chill until mixture is syrup consistency.

(continued on next page)

Beat remaining 3 ingredients in medium bowl until soft peaks form. Fold into thickened pineapple mixture. Cut raspberry, lime and lemon gelatin into 1/4 inch (6 mm) cubes. Fold into whipped cream mixture. Spread evenly over crust. Chill. Cuts into 15 pieces.

1 piece: 299 Calories; 18.3 g Total Fat (5.3 g Mono, 1 g Poly, 10.9 g Sat); 57 mg Cholesterol; 32 g Carbohydrate; trace Fibre; 3 g Protein; 203 mg Sodium

Pictured below.

Note: If you are using dessert topping in place of whipped cream, omit sugar and vanilla extract.

1. Pineapple Delight, page 72
2. Pink Lady, page 69
3. Layered Lemon, page 70
4. Peaches And Cream, page 64
5. Red Ribbon Delight, page 71
6. Broken Glass, page 66

A dreamy, creamy dessert everyone will want to taste. The crust sets off a mousse-like filling. No one will be too full to ask for more!

food fun

You know those times when nothing but chocolate will do? And when you get it, it just makes everything a little bit brighter? That's because there's more to this super soother than its out-of-this-world taste. Chocolate actually contains low levels of chemicals that create feelings of happiness. Some experts even suggest these feelings mimic the ones a person feels when in love. Which might just explain why almost everyone who tries chocolate, loves it!

Chilled Chocolate Dessert

CRUST

Large egg, fork-beaten	1	1
All-purpose flour	2 cups	500 mL
Brown sugar, packed	1/2 cup	125 mL
Butter (or hard margarine), softened	1/2 cup	125 mL
Baking powder	1 tsp.	5 mL
Vanilla extract	1 tsp.	5 mL
Salt	1/4 tsp.	1 mL

FILLING

Envelopes of dessert topping (not prepared)	2	2
Milk	2/3 cup	150 mL
Block of cream cheese, softened	8 oz.	250 g
Brown sugar, packed	1 cup	250 mL
Box of instant chocolate pudding powder (4-serving size)	1	1
Milk	1 1/2 cups	375 mL

Grated chocolate, for garnish

Crust: Mix all 7 ingredients in medium bowl until mixture resembles coarse crumbs. Press firmly in ungreased 9 x 13 inch (22 x 33 cm) pan. Bake in 350°F (175°C) oven for 12 to 15 minutes until edges are golden. Cool.

Filling: Beat dessert topping and first amount of milk in medium bowl until stiff peaks form. Set aside.

Using same beaters, beat cream cheese and brown sugar in separate medium bowl until smooth. Fold in half of dessert topping. Spread evenly over crust.

Beat pudding powder and second amount of milk in small bowl until smooth. Spread evenly over cream cheese mixture. Chill for about 5 minutes until set. Spread remaining dessert topping evenly over pudding mixture.

Garnish with chocolate. Chill until set. Cuts into 15 pieces.

1 piece: 386 Calories; 18.8 g Total Fat (3.5 g Mono, 0.6 g Poly, 13.7 g Sat); 46 mg Cholesterol; 51 g Carbohydrate; trace Fibre; 5 g Protein; 300 mg Sodium

Pictured on pages 3 and 65.

Pink Lady

Dressed up in pineapple, strawberries, marshmallows and a no-bake crust, this Pink Lady knows how to wow guests and family members alike.

CRUST

Butter (or hard margarine)	1/2 cup	125 mL
Graham cracker crumbs	2 cups	500 mL
Granulated sugar	1/3 cup	75 mL

FILLING

Reserved juice from pineapple (see Tip)	1 cup	250 mL
Large marshmallows	16	16
Box of raspberry jelly powder (gelatin)	3 oz.	85 g
Boiling water	1 cup	250 mL
Cold water	1 cup	250 mL
Can of pineapple chunks, drained and juice reserved, diced	14 oz.	398 mL
Sliced fresh strawberries	1 cup	250 mL
Whipping cream (or 1 envelope of dessert topping, prepared)	1 cup	250 mL
Slivered almonds	1/2 cup	125 mL
Vanilla extract	1/2 tsp.	2 mL

Medium unsweetened coconut, sprinkle

Crust: Melt butter in small saucepan on medium. Remove from heat. Add graham crumbs and sugar. Stir well. Reserve 1/3 cup (75 mL) for filling. Press remaining crumb mixture firmly into ungreased 8 × 8 inch (20 × 20 cm) pan.

Filling: Heat pineapple juice in large heavy saucepan on medium-low until hot, but not boiling. Add marshmallows. Heat and stir until melted. Cool, stirring occasionally.

Stir jelly powder into boiling water in small heatproof bowl until dissolved. Add cold water. Stir. Add to marshmallow mixture. Stir. Chill until mixture is syrup consistency.

Add pineapple and strawberries.

Beat whipping cream in medium bowl until soft peaks form. Fold in almonds and vanilla. Fold into gelatin mixture. Spread half of whipped cream mixture evenly over crust. Sprinkle with reserved crumb mixture. Spread remaining whipped cream mixture evenly over top.

Sprinkle with coconut. Chill until set. Cuts into 9 pieces.

1 piece: 417 Calories; 24.4 g Total Fat (8.0 g Mono, 2.2 g Poly, 12.7 g Sat); 61 mg Cholesterol; 48 g Carbohydrate; 2 g Fibre; 5 g Protein; 240 mg Sodium

Pictured on page 67.

tip

Not enough pineapple juice in your can of pineapple? Simply top up with water or store-bought pineapple juice to make 1 cup (250 mL).

A lemony tang gives this dessert its luscious, fresh taste—and it's large enough to serve at a wedding shower or ladies' luncheon.

about icing sugar

Fancy dessert presentations or your morning French toast just wouldn't be the same without it. And frostings? Impossible! But just what is icing sugar, anyway? Also called confectioner's or powdered sugar, icing sugar is nothing more than ordinary granulated sugar that has been ground into a fine powder, with the addition of a wee amount of cornstarch to prevent it from clumping.

Layered Lemon

CRUST

All-purpose flour	2 cups	500 mL
Butter (or hard margarine)	1 cup	250 mL
Finely chopped pecans	1 cup	250 mL

SECOND LAYER

Whipping cream (or 1 envelope of dessert topping, prepared)	1 cup	250 mL
Blocks of cream cheese (8 oz., 250 g, each), softened	2	2
Icing (confectioner's) sugar	1 cup	250 mL

THIRD LAYER

Envelopes of lemon pie filling (not instant), enough for 2 pies	2	2
Large eggs (see Note 1)	2	2

TOPPING

Whipping cream (or 2 envelopes of dessert topping, prepared), see Note 2	2 cups	500 mL
Granulated sugar	2 tbsp.	30 mL
Vanilla extract	1 tsp.	5 mL

Chopped pecans, for garnish

Crust: Measure flour into medium bowl. Cut in butter until mixture resembles coarse crumbs. Add pecans. Stir. Press firmly in ungreased 9 x 13 inch (22 x 33 cm) pan. Bake in 350°F (175°C) oven for about 15 minutes until golden. Cool.

Second Layer: Beat whipping cream in medium bowl until soft peaks form. Using same beaters, beat cream cheese and icing sugar in large bowl until smooth. Fold in whipped cream. Spread evenly over crust.

Third Layer: Prepare pie filling according to package directions, using 2 eggs. Cool, stirring often. Spread evenly over Second Layer.

Topping: Beat all 3 ingredients in medium bowl until soft peaks form. Spread evenly over Third Layer.

Garnish with pecans. Cuts into 24 pieces.

1 piece: 476 Calories; 31.1 g Total Fat (10.2 g Mono, 2.6 g Poly, 16.5 g Sat); 137 mg Cholesterol; 46 g Carbohydrate; 1 g Fibre; 6 g Protein; 156 mg Sodium

Pictured on page 67.

(continued on next page)

Note 1: Because this recipe doesn't use egg whites, use 2 whole eggs instead of the 4 yolks the package instructions call for.

Note 2: If you are using dessert topping in place of whipped cream, omit sugar and vanilla extract.

Red Ribbon Delight

Three layers of scintillating sweetness! This cool red treat is guaranteed to thrill kids and adults alike.

CRUST

All-purpose flour	1 1/4 cups	300 mL
Granulated sugar	2 tbsp.	30 mL
Butter (or hard margarine), softened	3/4 cup	175 mL

FILLING

Box of raspberry jelly powder (gelatin)	3 oz.	85 g
Boiling water	1 cup	250 mL
Container of frozen raspberries in syrup, partially thawed	15 oz.	425 g

TOPPING

Large marshmallows	16	16
Sour cream	1/2 cup	125 mL
Grenadine syrup	1 tbsp.	15 mL
Whipping cream (or 1 envelope of dessert topping, prepared)	1 cup	250 mL

Crust: Combine flour and sugar in medium bowl. Cut in butter until mixture resembles coarse crumbs. Press firmly in ungreased 9 × 9 inch (22 × 22 cm) pan. Bake in 350°F (175°C) oven for about 20 minutes until golden. Cool.

Filling: Stir jelly powder into boiling water in small heatproof bowl until dissolved. Add raspberries. Stir. Chill until mixture is syrup consistency. Pour over crust. Chill until set.

Topping: Melt marshmallows in sour cream in top of double boiler or heatproof bowl set over simmering water, stirring often, until smooth. Stir in grenadine syrup. Cool, stirring occasionally.

Beat whipping cream in medium bowl until soft peaks form. Fold into marshmallow mixture. Spread evenly over gelatin mixture. Chill. Cuts into 9 pieces.

1 piece: 460 Calories; 26.7 g Total Fat (7.3 g Mono, 1.0 g Poly, 16.8 g Sat); 80 mg Cholesterol; 53 g Carbohydrate; 2 g Fibre; 4 g Protein; 181 mg Sodium

Pictured on page 67.

Pineapple and whipped cream are the perfect team in this easy-to-make, scrumptious treat.

Pineapple Delight

CRUST

Butter (or hard margarine)	1/2 cup	125 mL
Graham cracker crumbs	2 cups	500 mL
Granulated sugar	1/4 cup	60 mL

FILLING

Icing (confectioner's) sugar	1 1/2 cups	375 mL
Butter (or hard margarine), softened	1/2 cup	125 mL
Large eggs (see Tip, page 83)	2	2
Whipping cream (or 1 envelope of dessert topping, prepared)	1 cup	250 mL
Can of crushed pineapple, well drained	19 oz.	540 mL

Crust: Melt butter in small saucepan on medium. Remove from heat. Add graham crumbs and sugar. Stir well. Reserve 1 cup (250 mL) for topping. Press remaining crumb mixture firmly into ungreased 9 × 13 (22 × 33 cm) pan. Bake in 350°F (175°C) oven for 10 minutes. Cool.

Filling: Beat icing sugar and butter in medium bowl until smooth. Add eggs, 1 at a time, beating well after each addition. Spread evenly over crust.

Using clean beaters, beat whipping cream in medium bowl until soft peaks form. Fold pineapple into whipped cream. Spread evenly over icing sugar mixture. Sprinkle with reserved crumb mixture. Chill until firm. Cuts into 15 pieces.

1 piece: 297 Calories; 19.5 g Total Fat (5.5 g Mono, 1.2 g Poly, 11.5 g Sat); 77 mg Cholesterol; 30 g Carbohydrate; 1 g Fibre; 2 g Protein; 168 mg Sodium

Pictured on page 67.

Cheesecake is a favourite of many. This raspberry version gets a kick from lemon and two different cheeses, making it even more rich and creamy.

Almond And Raspberry Cheesecake

CRUST

Ground almonds	3/4 cup	175 mL
Vanilla wafer crumbs	3/4 cup	175 mL
Butter (or hard margarine), melted	1/4 cup	60 mL

FILLING

Cream cheese, softened	8 oz.	250 g
Granulated sugar	1 cup	250 mL
Ricotta cheese	1 cup	250 mL

(continued on next page)

Large eggs	4	4
Egg yolk (large)	1	1
Sour cream	1 cup	250 mL
All purpose flour	3 tbsp.	50 mL
Grated lemon zest	1 tbsp.	15 mL
Fresh raspberries	1 1/4 cup	300 mL
Sliced almonds	1/3 cup	75 mL

Fresh raspberries, for garnish

Crust: Combine all 3 ingredients in medium bowl. Press firmly in bottom of greased 9 inch (22 cm) springform pan. Chill for 1 hour.

Filling: Beat first 3 ingredients in large bowl until smooth.

Add next 5 ingredients. Beat well. Pour over crust.

Sprinkle raspberries and almonds over top. Bake in 350°F (175°C) oven for about 1 hour until centre is almost set. Run knife around inside edge of pan to allow cheesecake to settle evenly. Let stand in pan on wire rack until cooled completely. Chill, covered, for at least 6 hours or overnight.

Garnish with raspberries. Cuts into 12 wedges.

1 wedge: 340 Calories; 22.7 g Total Fat (8.3 g Mono, 2.2 g Poly, 10.9 g Sat); 126 mg Cholesterol; 27 g Carbohydrate; 2 g Fibre; 9 g Protein; 154 mg Sodium

Pictured below.

tip

Don't confuse vanilla wafers with the popular ice cream wafer cookies. Vanilla wafers, although also found in the cookies aisle, come in a cardboard box and look like plain round cookies.

Almond And Raspberry Cheesecake, page 72

Orange and poppy seeds are commonly used in many European cakes. We've combined these traditional partners with yogurt to give a unique spin on traditional cheesecake.

Orange, Yogurt And Poppy Seed Cheesecake

CRUST

Graham cracker crumbs	2 cups	500 mL
Butter (or hard margarine), melted	1/2 cup	125 mL

FILLING

Envelopes of unflavoured gelatin (1/4 oz., 7 g, each)	2	2
Cold water	1/3 cup	75 mL
Blocks of cream cheese (8 oz., 250 g, each), softened	2	2
Plain yogurt	1 cup	250 mL
Granulated sugar	3/4 cup	175 mL
Orange juice	1/4 cup	60 mL
Grated orange zest (see Tip, page 56)	2 tbsp.	30 mL
Poppy seeds	3 tbsp.	50 mL

TOPPING

Orange juice	3/4 cup	175 mL
Cornstarch	1 1/2 tbsp.	25 mL
Granulated sugar	1 tbsp.	15 mL
Orange liqueur (optional)	1 tbsp.	15 mL

Orange slices, for garnish

Crust: Combine graham crumbs and butter in medium bowl. Press firmly in bottom and halfway up side of ungreased 9 inch (22 cm) springform pan. Chill for 1 hour.

Filling: Sprinkle gelatin over cold water in small saucepan. Let stand for 1 minute. Heat and stir on low until gelatin is dissolved. Cool.

Beat next 5 ingredients in large bowl until smooth. Add poppy seeds and gelatin mixture. Mix well. Spread evenly over crust. Chill, covered, for about 3 hours until set.

Topping: Combine first 3 ingredients in medium saucepan. Heat and stir on medium-high until boiling and thickened. Remove from heat.

Add liqueur. Stir. Let stand for 1 minute. Gently spread over filling. Chill until topping is set.

Garnish with orange slices. Cuts into 12 wedges.

1 wedge: 363 Calories; 24.6 g Total Fat (6.6 g Mono, 1.4 g Poly, 14.2 g Sat); 65 mg Cholesterol; 31 g Carbohydrate; 1 g Fibre; 5 g Protein; 265 mg Sodium

Pictured at right.

Pineapple Wink Pie

You'll be getting loads of winks after your dinner guests finish off their meal with this tart treat.

Can of crushed pineapple (with juice)	14 oz.	398 mL
Sour cream	1 cup	250 mL
Box of instant vanilla pudding powder (4-serving size)	1	1
Baked 9 inch (22 cm) pie shell (see Tip, page 60)		

TOPPING

Whipping cream (or 1 envelope of dessert topping, prepared), see Note	1 cup	250 mL
Granulated sugar	2 tsp.	10 mL
Vanilla extract	1/2 tsp.	2 mL

Combine first 3 ingredients in medium bowl. Spread evenly in pie shell. Chill until set.

Topping: Beat all 3 ingredients in medium bowl until soft peaks form. Spread evenly over pineapple mixture. Cuts into 8 wedges.

1 wedge: 312 Calories; 20.8 g Total Fat (7.0 g Mono, 1.2 g Poly, 11.4 g Sat); 50 mg Cholesterol; 29 g Carbohydrate; 1 g Fibre; 2 g Protein; 309 mg Sodium

Pictured below.

Note: If you are using dessert topping in place of whipped cream, omit sugar and vanilla extract.

Left: Orange, Yogurt And Poppy Seed Cheesecake, page 74
Right: Pineapple Wink Pie, above

Milk chocolate is asked to step aside while its cousin, white chocolate, takes the taste spotlight in this ravishing cheesecake. Rich and decadent.

food fun

So what, exactly, is up with white chocolate? It doesn't look like chocolate and it doesn't taste like it either. All for good reason—it isn't chocolate! It's actually a mixture of ingredients like cocoa butter, milk solids, vanilla and sugar.

Chocolate Raspberry Cheesecake

CRUST

Butter (or hard margarine), softened	1/2 cup	125 mL
Chocolate wafer crumbs	2 cups	500 mL

FILLING

Envelope of unflavoured gelatin (about 1 tbsp., 15 mL)	1/4 oz.	7 g
Cold water	1/3 cup	75 mL
White chocolate baking squares (1 oz., 28 g, each), cut up	12	12
Blocks of cream cheese (8 oz., 250 g, each), softened	2	2
Granulated sugar	1/2 cup	125 mL
Grated lemon zest	1 tsp.	5 mL
Lemon juice	1 tbsp.	15 mL

TOPPING

Apple juice	3/4 cup	175 mL
Cornstarch	1 1/2 tbsp.	25 mL
Granulated sugar	1 tbsp.	15 mL
Brandy (optional)	1 tbsp.	15 mL
Fresh raspberries	2 cups	500 mL

Crust: Melt butter in medium saucepan on medium. Remove from heat. Add wafer crumbs. Stir well. Press firmly in bottom and halfway up side of ungreased 9 inch (22 cm) springform pan. Chill for 1 hour.

Filling: Sprinkle gelatin over cold water in small saucepan. Let stand for 1 minute. Heat and stir on low until gelatin is dissolved. Cool.

Heat chocolate in small heavy saucepan on lowest heat, stirring often, until almost melted. Do not overheat. Remove from heat. Stir until smooth.

Beat next 4 ingredients in large bowl until smooth. Add gelatin mixture and chocolate. Mix well. Spread evenly over crust. Chill, covered, for about 3 hours until set.

Topping: Combine first 3 ingredients in separate medium saucepan. Heat and stir on medium-high for about 2 minutes until boiling and thickened. Remove from heat.

(continued on next page)

Stir in brandy. Let stand for 1 minute. Gently spread over filling.

Arrange raspberries, open-end down, over top. Chill for about 1 hour until topping is set. Cuts into 12 wedges.

1 wedge: 492 Calories; 32.6 g Total Fat (9.2 g Mono, 1.9 g Poly, 19.4 g Sat); 68 mg Cholesterol; 46 g Carbohydrate; 2 g Fibre; 6 g Protein; 302 mg Sodium

Pictured below.

*It's margarita mania! The strawberry
filling takes centre stage in this
chocolate-crusted pie. Daydream
about long summer days and enjoy!*

food fun

Talk about a drink with a
complicated history! There are
several conflicting theories as
to the origin of the margarita.
Depending on who you ask,
it was created in 1938 (or 1948,
or 1942) in Tijuana (or Acapulco,
or Juárez), and is named after
a showgirl (or the socialite) who
invented it! It's unlikely history
will ever agree on a single origin,
but don't let that stop you from
enjoying this classic combination.

Strawberry Margarita Pie

Box of strawberry jelly powder (gelatin)	3 oz.	85 g
Boiling water	3/4 cup	175 mL
Lime juice	1/2 cup	125 mL
Grated lime zest	1 tsp.	5 mL
Frozen whipped topping, thawed (or whipped cream)	2 cups	500 mL
Chocolate crumb crust (9 inch, 22 cm, diameter)	1	1

Halved fresh strawberries, for garnish

Stir jelly powder into boiling water in large heatproof bowl until dissolved.

Add lime juice and lime zest. Stir. Chill for about 45 minutes, stirring occasionally, until very thick and starting to set. Beat for about 3 minutes until fluffy.

Fold in whipped topping. Spread evenly in crumb crust. Chill for about 2 hours until set.

Garnish with strawberries. Cuts into 8 wedges.

1 wedge: 193 Calories; 8.5 g Total Fat (0 g Mono, 0 g Poly, 5 g Sat); 0 mg Cholesterol; 29 g Carbohydrate; 1 g Fibre; 2 g Protein; 164 mg Sodium

Pictured on page 81.

*Satiny smooth on the palate with a
flavour explosion of pink lemonade—
who would have thought dessert could
be so sensational?*

Pink Velvet Pie

Can of sweetened condensed milk	11 oz.	300 mL
Block of cream cheese, softened	8 oz.	250 g
Frozen concentrated pink lemonade, thawed	3/4 cup	175 mL
Frozen whipped topping, thawed (or whipped cream)	2 cups	500 mL
Chocolate crumb crust (9 inch, 22 cm, diameter)	1	1

Beat first 3 ingredients in medium bowl until smooth.

Fold in whipped topping.

Pour into crumb crust. Chill for about 2 hours until firm. Cuts into 8 wedges.

(continued on next page)

1 wedge: 424 Calories; 21.8 g Total Fat (3.7 g Mono, 0.5 g Poly, 13.4 g Sat); 44 mg Cholesterol; 53 g Carbohydrate; 1 g Fibre; 6 g Protein; 254 mg Sodium

Pictured on page 81.

Coconut Cream Pie

Milk	2 1/4 cups	550 mL
Granulated sugar	2/3 cup	150 mL
All-purpose flour	1/2 cup	125 mL
Salt	1/4 tsp.	1 mL
Egg yolks	3	3
Butter (or hard margarine)	2 tbsp.	30 mL
Vanilla extract	1 tsp.	5 mL
Shredded coconut	1 cup	250 mL
Baked 9 inch (22 cm) pie shell (see Tip, page 60)		
TOPPING		
Whipping cream (or 1 envelope of dessert topping, prepared), see Note	1 cup	250 mL
Granulated sugar	1 tbsp.	15 mL
Vanilla extract	3/4 tsp.	4 mL
Shredded coconut, toasted (see Tip, page 48)	1/3 cup	75 mL

Rich and exotic, this favourite pie is as temptingly delicious as it is straightforward to make. Your guests will rave about your talent in the kitchen!

Measure milk into large saucepan. Bring to a boil on medium. Combine next 3 ingredients in small bowl. Slowly add to milk, stirring constantly with whisk until smooth. Heat and stir until boiling and thickened.

Combine next 3 ingredients in small bowl. Slowly add about 1/2 cup (125 mL) hot milk mixture, stirring constantly. Slowly add egg yolk mixture to remaining hot milk mixture. Heat and stir until boiling and thickened. Remove from heat.

Add coconut. Stir. Let stand for 15 minutes. Spread evenly in pie shell. Cover with plastic wrap directly on surface to prevent skin from forming. Chill until firm.

Topping: Beat first 3 ingredients in medium bowl until soft peaks form. Spread evenly over coconut mixture. Sprinkle with coconut. Cuts into 8 wedges.

1 wedge: 367 Calories; 28.5 g Total Fat (7.6 g Mono, 1.5 g Poly, 17.6 g Sat); 120 mg Cholesterol; 23 g Carbohydrate; 2 g Fibre; 6 g Protein; 247 mg Sodium

Note: If you are using dessert topping in place of whipped cream, omit sugar and vanilla extract.

Chocolate brown and mint green colours showcase the cool flavours of this minty delicacy.

Grasshopper Pie

CRUST		
Butter (or hard margarine)	1/3 cup	75 mL
Chocolate wafer crumbs	1 1/4 cups	300 mL
FILLING		
Milk	1/2 cup	125 mL
Large marshmallows	24	24
Mint liqueur, green	1/4 cup	60 mL
Chocolate liqueur, clear	2 tbsp.	30 mL
Whipping cream (or 1 envelope of dessert topping, prepared)	1 cup	250 mL

Crust: Melt butter in small saucepan on medium. Remove from heat. Add wafer crumbs. Stir well. Reserve 2 tbsp. (30 mL) for topping. Press firmly in bottom and up side of 9 inch (22 cm) pie plate. Chill.

Filling: Heat milk in large heavy saucepan on medium-low until hot, but not boiling. Add marshmallows. Heat and stir until melted. Cool, stirring occasionally.

Stir in mint and chocolate liqueur.

Beat whipping cream in medium bowl until soft peaks form. Fold into marshmallow mixture. Spread evenly in crust. Sprinkle with reserved crumb mixture. Chill. Cuts into 8 wedges.

1 wedge: 346 Calories; 20.7 g Total Fat (5.9 g Mono, 1.4 g Poly, 12.1 g Sat); 59 mg Cholesterol; 34 g Carbohydrate; 1 g Fibre; 3 g Protein; 192 mg Sodium

Pictured at right.

1. Orange Chiffon Pie, page 83
2. Grasshopper Pie, above
3. Pink Velvet Pie, page 78
4. Strawberry Margarita Pie, page 78

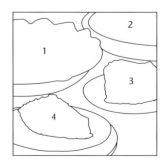

Chocolate and coffee is one of the greatest combinations ever invented—and you'll agree after getting your fill of this exquisite pie. If you want to lighten this up a bit, it's just as good without the topping.

food fun

You're making a meringue-based dessert, and the recipe calls for egg whites, sugar, and... cream of *what*? This mysterious-sounding ingredient is derived from crystals that form inside wine barrels. It's used to stabilize egg whites and add creaminess to candy and frostings. And, as an added bonus, it's fabulous for cleaning stained aluminum pots! Just fill the pot with 2 tbsp (30 mL) cream of tartar and 1 quart (1 L) water, then let it boil for 10 minutes, wash as usual and it'll be good as new! Cream of tartar is also good for cleaning porcelain—just sprinkle some on a damp cloth and polish away.

Chocolate Mocha Chiffon Pie

Packages of unflavoured gelatin (1/4 oz., 7 g, each)	2	2
Cold water	1/2 cup	125 mL
Milk	1 3/4 cups	425 mL
Cocoa, sifted if lumpy	1/2 cup	125 mL
Butter (or hard margarine)	2 tbsp.	30 mL
Egg yolks (large)	2	2
Granulated sugar	1/2 cup	125 mL
Instant coffee granules	3 tbsp.	50 mL
Vanilla extract	1 tsp.	5 mL
Egg whites (large), room temperature (see Tip, page 83)	2	2
Cream of tartar	1/4 tsp.	1 mL
Granulated sugar	1/2 cup	125 mL
Whipping cream (or 1 envelope of dessert topping, prepared)	1 cup	250 mL
Baked 9 inch (22 cm) pie shell (see Tip, page 60)		
TOPPING		
Whipping cream (or 1 envelope of dessert topping, prepared), see Note	1 cup	250 mL
Granulated sugar	2 tsp.	10 mL
Vanilla extract	1/2 tsp.	2 mL

Sprinkle gelatin over cold water in medium saucepan. Let stand for 1 minute. Heat and stir on low until gelatin is dissolved.

Add next 3 ingredients. Heat and stir on medium until boiling.

Combine next 4 ingredients in small bowl. Slowly add about 1/2 cup (125 mL) hot milk mixture, stirring constantly. Slowly add egg yolk mixture to remaining hot milk mixture. Heat and stir until boiling and thickened. Chill until mixture is syrup consistency.

Beat egg whites and cream of tartar in medium bowl until soft peaks form. Slowly add second amount of sugar, 1 tbsp. (15 mL) at a time, beating constantly until stiff peaks form and sugar is dissolved. Fold into gelatin mixture.

(continued on next page)

Beat whipping cream in medium bowl until soft peaks form. Fold into gelatin mixture. Spread evenly in pie shell. Chill.

Topping: Beat all 3 ingredients in same medium bowl until soft peaks form. Spread evenly over mocha mixture. Cuts into 8 wedges.

1 wedge: 462 Calories; 31.3 g Total Fat (10.2 g Mono, 1.7 g Poly, 17.6 g Sat); 133 mg Cholesterol; 42 g Carbohydrate; 2 g Fibre; 7 g Protein; 192 mg Sodium

Note: If you are using dessert topping in place of whipped cream, omit sugar and vanilla extract.

Orange Chiffon Pie

Package of unflavoured gelatin (about 1 tbsp., 15 mL)	1/4 oz.	7 g
Cold water	1 cup	250 mL
Granulated sugar	1/2 cup	125 mL
Salt	1/8 tsp.	0.5 mL
Egg yolks (large), fork-beaten	3	3
Frozen concentrated orange juice, thawed	3/4 cup	175 mL
Egg whites (large), room temperature (see Tip)	3	3
Granulated sugar	1/4 cup	60 mL
Baked 9 inch (22 cm) pie shell (see Tip, page 60)		

Mighty tall on orange taste and a perfect after-meal accompaniment, this pie is a slice of heaven. Garnish with an orange twist.

tip

When preparing recipes that use raw egg, make sure to use fresh, uncracked, clean Grade A eggs. Pregnant women, young children or the elderly are not advised to eat anything containing raw egg.

Sprinkle gelatin over cold water in small saucepan. Let stand for 1 minute. Add first amount of sugar and salt. Heat and stir on low until gelatin and sugar are dissolved.

Slowly add about 1/3 cup (75 mL) hot gelatin mixture to egg yolks in small bowl, stirring constantly. Slowly add egg yolk mixture to remaining hot gelatin mixture, stirring constantly until boiling and thickened. Cool slightly.

Add concentrated orange juice. Stir. Chill until mixture is syrup consistency.

Beat egg whites in large bowl until soft peaks form. Add second amount of sugar, 1 tbsp. (15 mL) at a time, beating constantly until stiff peaks form and sugar is dissolved. Fold into gelatin mixture. Spread evenly in pie shell. Chill. Cuts into 8 wedges.

1 wedge: 224 Calories; 7.1 g Total Fat (3.3 g Mono, 0.9 g Poly, 2.3 g Sat); 71 mg Cholesterol; 37 g Carbohydrate; trace Fibre; 4 g Protein; 164 mg Sodium

Pictured on page 81.

Drumstick Cake

CRUST

Butter (or hard margarine)	1/4 cup	60 mL
Smooth peanut butter	3 tbsp.	50 mL
Chocolate wafer crumbs	1 1/2 cups	375 mL
Finely chopped pecans	1/2 cup	125 mL

FILLING

Block of cream cheese, softened	8 oz.	250 g
Granulated sugar	1/2 cup	125 mL
Smooth peanut butter	1/2 cup	125 mL
Large eggs (see Tip, page 83)	2	2
Milk	2 tbsp.	30 mL
Vanilla extract	1 1/2 tsp.	7 mL
Frozen whipped topping, thawed (or whipped cream)	4 cups	1 L

TOPPING

Butterscotch ice cream topping	1/4 cup	60 mL
Chocolate ice cream topping	1/4 cup	60 mL

Crust: Melt butter in medium saucepan on medium. Remove from heat. Stir in peanut butter until smooth. Add wafer crumbs and pecans. Stir well. Reserve 1/2 cup (125 mL) for topping. Press firmly in ungreased 9 × 13 inch (22 × 33 cm) pan.

Filling: Beat first 3 ingredients in large bowl until smooth. Add eggs, 1 at a time, beating well after each addition. Add milk and vanilla. Mix well.

Fold in whipped topping. Spread evenly over crust.

Topping: Drizzle butterscotch and chocolate ice cream toppings over filling. Sprinkle with reserved crumb mixture. Freeze, covered, for at least 6 hours or overnight. Let stand at room temperature for about 10 minutes before cutting. Cuts into 15 pieces.

1 piece: 342 Calories; 23.7 g Total Fat (7.6 g Mono, 3.4 g Poly, 11.7 g Sat); 50 mg Cholesterol; 29 g Carbohydrate; 1 g Fibre; 6 g Protein; 224 mg Sodium

Pictured at right.

Left: Drumstick Cake, above
Right: Frozen Mocha Cheesecake, page 86

This awesome, rich dessert is a working person's dream. Just cut a slice or two and put the rest back into the freezer—a treat in no time.

about graham crackers

When you think of graham crackers, you probably think of s'mores, cheesecake and other desserts. What you may not know is that this dessert staple was originally conceived as a health food! Crackers made from graham flour, a coarse whole-wheat flour, were created in the 1830s by Rev. Sylvester Graham, an early proponent of healthful eating. Alas, modern graham crackers and crumbs are made mostly of white flour and are far sweeter than the originals. Tasty, yes, but nutritious? We think not.

Frozen Mocha Cheesecake

CRUST
Butter (or hard margarine)	1/2 cup	125 mL
Graham cracker crumbs	1 1/2 cups	375 mL
Granulated sugar	1/4 cup	60 mL
Cocoa, sifted if lumpy	1/4 cup	60 mL

FILLING
Block of cream cheese, softened	8 oz.	250 g
Can of sweetened condensed milk	11 oz.	300 mL
Chocolate ice cream topping	2/3 cup	150 mL
Instant coffee granules	1 tbsp.	15 mL
Hot water	1 tsp.	5 mL
Whipping cream (or 1 envelope of dessert topping, prepared)	1 cup	250 mL

Crust: Melt butter in medium saucepan on medium. Remove from heat. Add next 3 ingredients. Stir well. Reserve 1/2 cup (125 mL) for topping. Press firmly in bottom and 1 inch (2.5 cm) up side of ungreased 9 inch (22 cm) springform pan.

Filling: Beat cream cheese in medium bowl until smooth. Add condensed milk and ice cream topping. Mix well.

Dissolve coffee granules in hot water. Add to cream cheese mixture. Stir.

Beat whipping cream in medium bowl until soft peaks form. Fold into cream cheese mixture. Spread evenly in crust. Sprinkle with reserved crumb mixture. Freeze until firm. Cuts into 8 wedges.

1 wedge: 585 Calories; 37.7 g Total Fat (10.5 g Mono, 1.9 g Poly, 22.5 g Sat); 113 mg Cholesterol; 58 g Carbohydrate; 2 g Fibre; 8 g Protein; 334 mg Sodium

Pictured on page 85.

White Chocolate Orange Chill

White chocolate and orange—how could anyone resist this tantalizing combination? They won't be able to. We're certain.

CRUST

Butter (or hard margarine)	1/3 cup	75 mL
Chocolate wafer crumbs	1 1/2 cups	375 mL

FILLING

Granulated sugar	1/2 cup	125 mL
Orange juice	1/2 cup	125 mL
Frozen concentrated orange juice	1/4 cup	60 mL
Orange liqueur (or orange juice)	1/4 cup	60 mL
Lemon juice	1 tsp.	5 mL
Salt, just a pinch		
Envelope of unflavoured gelatin (about 1 tbsp., 15 mL)	1/4 oz.	7 g
Cold water	1/4 cup	60 mL
Envelope of dessert topping (prepared), or 2 cups (500 mL) whipped cream	1	1
Grated white chocolate	1/2 cup	125 mL

White chocolate curls, for garnish
Orange slices, for garnish
Whipped cream, for garnish
Chocolate chips, for garnish

Crust: Melt butter in medium saucepan on medium. Remove from heat. Add wafer crumbs. Stir well. Press firmly in bottom and 1 inch (2.5 cm) up side of ungreased 8 inch (20 cm) springform pan. Chill.

Filling: Combine first 6 ingredients in large bowl.

Sprinkle gelatin over cold water in small saucepan. Let stand for 1 minute. Heat and stir on low until gelatin is dissolved. Add to orange juice mixture. Stir until sugar is dissolved. Cool slightly.

Fold in dessert topping until no white streaks remain.

Gently fold in chocolate. Spread evenly in crust. Freeze until set.

Garnish with chocolate curls, orange slices, whipped cream and chocolate chips. Cuts into 12 wedges.

1 wedge: 235 Calories; 11.0 g Total Fat (2.8 g Mono, 0.9 g Poly, 6.6 g Sat); 16 mg Cholesterol; 31 g Carbohydrate; 1 g Fibre; 2 g Protein; 135 mg Sodium

Pictured on page 89.

Save your money and try making this splendid cake for the next birthday party in your family. No one will mind getting a year older with a cake like this!

variations

Customize your Ice Cream Cake by using your favourite flavours of ice cream or by omitting the brown sugar and using two crushed Skor, Heath or Crispy Crunch bars for extra oomph. Or you can drizzle your favourite ice cream topping over one or both crumb layers.

Ice Cream Cake

Butter (or hard margarine)	3/4 cup	175 mL
Chocolate wafer crumbs	3 cups	750 mL
Brown sugar, packed	1/3 cup	75 mL
Chocolate ice cream, softened	8 cups	2 L
Strawberry ice cream, softened	8 cups	2 L
Frozen whipped topping, thawed	2 cups	500 mL
Halved fresh strawberries, for garnish		
Grated chocolate, for garnish		

Melt butter in medium saucepan on medium. Remove from heat. Add wafer crumbs and brown sugar. Stir well. Press 1/3 of crumb mixture firmly in bottom of ungreased 10 inch (25 cm) springform pan.

Spoon chocolate ice cream over crumb layer. Sprinkle with half of remaining crumb mixture. Press down lightly. Freeze until firm.

Spoon strawberry ice cream over second crumb layer. Sprinkle with remaining crumb mixture. Press down lightly. Freeze until firm. Let stand at room temperature for 10 minutes. Run knife around inside edge of pan to loosen sides.

Pipe whipped topping over top in decorative pattern. Freeze until set.

Garnish with strawberries and chocolate. Cuts into 20 wedges.

1 wedge: 583 Calories; 38.0 g Total Fat (2.6 g Mono, 1.0 g Poly, 23.4 g Sat); 186 mg Cholesterol; 53 g Carbohydrate; 2 g Fibre; 8 g Protein; 251 mg Sodium

Pictured at right.

Top: Ice Cream Cake, above
Bottom: White Chocolate Orange Chill, page 87

You'll want to look at this cake as much as you'll want to eat it. A layer of miniature jelly rolls is topped with tart mango and raspberry gelato. The vibrant colours and textures complement each other beautifully.

food fun

Have you read about Italy and its amazing gelato, and wanted to give this European treat a try? Well, technically speaking, "gelato" is Italian for "ice cream." The difference between gelato and traditional ice cream is that gelato contains less air, giving it a dense, creamy texture and intense flavour. Often it is made with milk, rather than cream, making it lower in fat than its North American counterpart.

Layered Gelato Cake

Packages of jam-filled jelly rolls (3/4 lb., 340 g, each), 6 per package	2	2
Raspberry jam	1/2 cup	125 mL
MANGO GELATO		
Half-and-half cream	1 1/4 cups	300 mL
Granulated sugar	1/2 cup	125 mL
Unflavoured gelatin (half of 1/4 oz., 7 g, envelope)	1 1/2 tsp.	7 mL
Salt, sprinkle		
Can of sliced mango in syrup, drained	14 oz.	398 mL
Egg white (large), room temperature (see Tip, page 83)	1	1
RASPBERRY GELATO		
Half-and-half cream	1 1/4 cups	300 mL
Granulated sugar	1/2 cup	125 mL
Unflavoured gelatin (half of 1/4 oz., 7 g, envelope)	1 1/2 tsp.	7 mL
Salt, sprinkle		
Fresh raspberries (or whole frozen, thawed, with juice)	2 1/2 cups	625 mL
Egg white (large), room temperature (see Tip, page 83)	1	1
Fresh raspberries, for garnish		

Cut jelly rolls crosswise into 3/4 inch (2 cm) slices. Set aside 14 slices. Arrange remaining slices in bottom of ungreased 10 inch (25 cm) springform pan. Arrange reserved slices around inside edge of pan. Spread jam evenly over bottom layer. Freeze.

Mango Gelato: Combine first 4 ingredients in small saucepan. Let stand for 1 minute. Heat and stir on low until sugar and gelatin are dissolved. Cool slightly.

Put mango into blender or food processor. Process until smooth. Add to gelatin mixture. Stir.

(continued on next page)

Beat egg white in medium bowl until soft peaks form. Fold mango mixture into egg white. Spread evenly in ungreased 9 × 9 inch (22 × 22 cm) pan. Freeze, uncovered, for about 1 hour until slushy. Transfer to separate medium bowl. Beat on high until foamy and light. Makes about 2 1/4 cups (550 mL) gelato. Spread evenly over jam. Freeze, covered, for 2 hours.

Raspberry Gelato: Combine first 4 ingredients in small saucepan. Let stand for 1 minute. Heat and stir on low until sugar and gelatin are dissolved. Cool slightly.

Put raspberries into blender or food processor. Process until smooth. Strain through sieve into small bowl. Discard seeds. Add to gelatin mixture. Stir.

Beat egg white in medium bowl until soft peaks form. Fold raspberry mixture into egg white. Spread evenly in separate ungreased 9 × 9 inch (22 × 22 cm) pan. Freeze, uncovered, for about 1 hour until slushy. Transfer to separate medium bowl. Beat on high until foamy and light. Makes about 2 cups (500 mL) gelato. Spread evenly over Mango Gelato. Freeze, covered, for at least 8 hours or overnight. Let stand at room temperature for 30 minutes before cutting.

Garnish individual servings with raspberries. Cuts into 12 wedges.

1 wedge: 408 Calories; 13.9 g Total Fat (6.3 g Mono, 1.4 g Poly, 5.4 g Sat); 51 mg Cholesterol; 68 g Carbohydrate; 3 g Fibre; 6 g Protein; 236 mg Sodium

Pictured below.

An angelic-looking treat that will beat the heat—and with the many flavours captured within, it's sure to keep your taste buds entertained.

Tri-Colour Angel Roll

Box of angel food cake mix	15 oz.	430 g
Lemonade	1 1/4 cups	300 mL
Grated lemon zest	1 1/2 tsp.	7 mL
Flaked coconut, toasted (see Tip, page 48)	1 cup	250 mL
Granulated sugar	1/4 cup	60 mL
Raspberry sherbet, softened	2 cups	500 mL
Lime sherbet, softened	2 cups	500 mL
Orange sherbet, softened	2 cups	500 mL

Line bottom of ungreased 11 x 17 inch (28 x 43 cm) baking sheet with sides with parchment (or waxed) paper. Prepare cake mix according to package directions, using lemonade instead of water.

Fold in lemon zest. Spread evenly in prepared pan. Bake in 400°F (205°C) oven for about 15 minutes until golden and wooden pick inserted in centre comes out clean. Let stand in pan on wire rack for 5 minutes. Run knife around inside edges of pan to loosen cake. Spread large tea towel on work surface. Cover with sheet of waxed paper.

Sprinkle coconut and sugar on waxed paper. Invert cake onto coconut mixture. Carefully peel off and discard parchment paper from bottom of cake. Roll up from short end, with towel and waxed paper. Let stand until cool. Unroll cake.

Spoon and spread alternating colours of sherbet in 6 crosswise rows on cake, to within 1 inch (2.5 cm) of each edge. Pack down gently. Smooth sherbet together to fill in any spaces. Roll up gently from short end, using waxed paper as a guide. Place roll, seam-side down, on serving plate. Wrap with plastic wrap. Freeze for at least 8 hours or overnight. Trim ends. Cuts into 10 slices.

1 slice: 415 Calories; 5.3 g Total Fat (0.5 g Mono, 0.2 g Poly, 4.0 g Sat); 2 mg Cholesterol; 89 g Carbohydrate; 3 g Fibre; 5 g Protein; 347 mg Sodium

Pictured at right.

A wonderful, tropical-tasting medley of ice cream, mango and macadamia nuts sandwiched between cookies with a hint of orange and a satisfying crunch. You'll have lots of offers to help you make and eat this fun treat.

Mango Macadamia Sandwich

COOKIES

All-purpose flour	1 1/2 cups	375 mL
Icing (confectioner's) sugar	3/4 cup	175 mL
Finely grated orange zest	2 tsp.	10 mL
Vanilla extract	1 tsp.	5 mL
Ground cinnamon	3/4 tsp.	4 mL
Cold butter (or hard margarine), cut up	1/2 cup	125 mL
Egg yolks (large), fork-beaten	2	2

FILLING

Vanilla ice cream, softened	2 cups	500 mL
Can of sliced mango in syrup, drained and chopped	14 oz.	398 mL
Macadamia nuts, chopped and toasted (see Tip, page 48)	1/2 cup	125 mL

Cookies: Combine first 5 ingredients in large bowl. Cut in butter until mixture resembles coarse crumbs.

Add egg yolks. Mix until soft dough forms. Roll out on lightly floured surface to 1/4 inch (6 mm) thickness. Cut out circles with lightly floured 3 inch (7.5 cm) round fluted cookie cutter. Arrange about 1 inch (2.5 cm) apart on lightly greased cookie sheets. Bake in 350°F (175°C) oven for 10 to 15 minutes until golden. Let stand on cookie sheets for 5 minutes. Remove cookies from cookie sheets and place on wire racks to cool. Makes about 16 cookies.

Filling: Combine all 3 ingredients in medium bowl. Line 9 x 9 inch (22 x 22 cm) pan with waxed paper, leaving 2 inch (5 cm) overhang on 2 sides. Spread ice cream mixture evenly in pan. Freeze, covered, for about 1 hour until firm. Holding waxed paper, remove ice cream from pan. Cut out circles with 2 1/2 inch (6.4 cm) round cookie cutter, as close together as possible. Place 1 ice cream round on 1 cookie. Cover with another cookie. Repeat with remaining cookies and ice cream rounds. Freeze. Makes 8 sandwiches.

1 sandwich: 469 Calories; 28.0 g Total Fat (8.5 g Mono, 0.8 g Poly, 14.1 g Sat); 137 mg Cholesterol; 50 g Carbohydrate; 2 g Fibre; 6 g Protein; 119 mg Sodium

Pictured on page 3 and at right.

Peachsicle Slice

Orange juice	2 cups	500 mL
Chopped dried peach	1/2 cup	125 mL
Can of sliced peaches in juice (with juice)	14 oz.	398 mL
Low-fat peach yogurt	1/2 cup	125 mL
Vanilla ice cream, softened	1 1/2 cups	375 mL

Put orange juice and dried peach into blender or food processor. Process until smooth.

Add peaches with juice and yogurt. Process until smooth. Spread half of peach mixture evenly in plastic wrap-lined 9 × 5 × 3 inch (22 × 12.5 × 7.5 cm) loaf pan. Freeze for about 3 hours until firm. Chill remaining peach mixture.

Spread ice cream evenly over frozen peach mixture. Stir remaining peach mixture. Spread evenly over ice cream. Freeze, covered, for at least 6 hours or overnight. Invert onto cutting board. Discard plastic wrap. Cuts into 8 slices.

1 slice: 204 Calories; 7.1 g Total Fat (trace Mono, 0.1 g Poly, 4.3 g Sat); 46 mg Cholesterol; 31 g Carbohydrate; 2 g Fibre; 4 g Protein; 38 mg Sodium

Pictured on page 3 and below.

Golden layers of peachy frozen yogurt sandwich vanilla ice cream. Serve with fresh berries or berry coulis.

tip

Dip your knife in hot water before cutting frozen desserts.

Left: Mango Macadamia Sandwich, page 94
Right: Peachsicle Slice, above

You won't be sugar-coating it when you tell your family and friends just how great this dessert is. Sure to become one of everyone's favourites.

Ice Cream Toffee Slice

CRUST

Butter (or hard margarine)	3/4 cup	175 mL
Chocolate wafer crumbs	2 1/2 cups	625 mL
Granulated sugar	1/4 cup	60 mL

FILLING

Vanilla ice cream (see Note)	2 quarts	2 L
Butterscotch (or caramel) ice cream topping	1 cup	250 mL
Frozen whipped topping, thawed	1 cup	250 mL

Crust: Melt butter in medium saucepan on medium. Remove from heat. Add wafer crumbs and sugar. Stir well. Reserve 1 cup (250 mL) for topping. Press remaining crumb mixture firmly in ungreased 9 × 13 inch (22 × 33 cm) pan.

Filling: Cut ice cream crosswise into 3/4 inch (2 cm) thick slices. Arrange slices in single layer over crust, cutting to fit.

Drizzle with ice cream topping. Sprinkle with 2/3 cup (150 mL) reserved crumb mixture.

Spread or pipe whipped topping over top. Sprinkle with remaining crumb mixture. Freeze until firm. Cuts into 15 pieces.

1 piece: 528 Calories; 32.0 g Total Fat (3.3 g Mono, 1.1 g Poly, 19.3 g Sat); 152 mg Cholesterol; 54 g Carbohydrate; 1 g Fibre; 7 g Protein; 309 mg Sodium

Pictured at right.

Note: A block of ice cream works best for this recipe. If you don't have a block, use 8 cups (2 L) softened vanilla ice cream and spread evenly over crust, packing down lightly.

This scrumptious snack will have your friends and family up and running when you call them in for a treat.

Ice Cream Sandwiches

Mashed banana (about 1 medium)	1/2 cup	125 mL
Peanut butter	2 tbsp.	30 mL
Chocolate chips	1 tbsp.	15 mL
Whole graham crackers	18	18
Vanilla ice cream, softened	2 cups	500 mL

(continued on next page)

Combine first 3 ingredients in small microwave-safe bowl. Microwave, covered, on high (100%) for 45 to 60 seconds until chocolate chips are softened. Do not overheat. Stir until smooth.

Spread banana mixture on crackers. Arrange 9 crackers, spread-side up, in 8 × 8 inch (20 × 20 cm) pan to cover bottom.

Spread ice cream over crackers in pan. Arrange remaining crackers, spread-side down, over ice cream. Press down gently. Freeze, covered, for at least 6 hours or overnight. Cut between crackers. Makes 9 sandwiches.

1 sandwich: 217 Calories; 11.6 g Total Fat (1.7 g Mono, 0.7 g Poly, 5.8 g Sat); 53 mg Cholesterol; 24 g Carbohydrate; 1 g Fibre; 4 g Protein; 133 mg Sodium

Pictured below.

Left: Ice Cream Sandwiches, page 96
Right: Ice Cream Toffee Slice, page 96

variation

For a lower fat alternative, use frozen yogurt instead of ice cream.

Anything with ice cream spells H-I-T in our book. This is our classic version of the all-time kid pleaser.

Sundae Dessert

CRUST		
Maple-flavoured sandwich cookies (half of 12 1/2 oz., 350 g, package)	11	11
FILLING		
Butterscotch ripple ice cream, softened	4 cups	1 L
Chocolate-covered buttery toffee bars (Skor or Heath), 1 1/2 oz. (39 g), each, coarsely chopped	4	4
Chocolate ice cream topping	1 cup	250 mL
Maple walnut ice cream, softened	4 cups	1 L
TOPPING		
Envelope of dessert topping (prepared)	1	1
Caramel (or butterscotch) ice cream topping	1/2 cup	125 mL
Chopped walnuts, toasted (see Tip, page 48)	1/4 cup	60 mL
Chocolate-covered buttery toffee bar (Skor or Heath), 1 1/2 oz. (39 g), finely chopped	1/2	1/2

Crust: Put cookies into food processor. Process with on/off motion until coarse crumbs form. Spread evenly in ungreased 9 x 13 inch (22 x 33 cm) pan. Pack down lightly.

Filling: Spoon butterscotch ripple ice cream over crust. Pack down lightly.

Sprinkle with toffee bar. Drizzle with chocolate ice cream topping. Freeze for about 2 hours until firm.

Spoon maple walnut ice cream over ice cream topping. Pack down lightly.

Topping: Spread or pipe dessert topping evenly over ice cream.

Drizzle caramel ice cream topping over top. Sprinkle with walnuts and toffee bar. Freeze, covered, for about 2 hours until firm. Let stand at room temperature for 20 minutes before cutting. Cuts into 25 pieces.

1 piece: 323 Calories; 18.3 g Total Fat (0.8 g Mono, 0.7 g Poly, 9.6 g Sat); 77 mg Cholesterol; 36 g Carbohydrate; trace Fibre; 5 g Protein; 120 mg Sodium

Pictured at right and on back cover.

food fun

Is there anything more hotly contested than the origins of popular cocktails? We've done the research and we can honestly tell you, no there isn't. And the piña colada is no exception. A blend of coconut cream, pineapple juice and rum, it's become a popular flavouring for everything sweet from ice cream to candy. One great contender for best origin concerns a bartender in Puerto Rico who substituted hollowed-out pineapples when the coconuts used to serve a coconut cocktail became unavailable. As the story goes, those who tasted the pineapple concoction couldn't get enough of the delicious tropical flavour, and the piña colada was born.

Piña Colada Pie

SHORTBREAD CRUST

All-purpose flour	1 1/2 cups	375 mL
Granulated sugar	2 tbsp.	30 mL
Cold butter (or hard margarine), cut up	3/4 cup	175 mL

FILLING

Block of cream cheese, softened	8 oz.	250 g
Granulated sugar	1/2 cup	125 mL
Rum extract	1 tsp.	5 mL
Can of crushed pineapple, drained	14 oz.	398 mL
Corn syrup	1/4 cup	60 mL
Coconut extract	1 tsp.	5 mL
Whipping cream	1 cup	250 mL

TOPPING

Whipping cream	1/2 cup	125 mL
Granulated sugar	1 tsp.	5 mL
Vanilla extract	1/4 tsp.	1 mL
Maraschino cherries	8	8

Shortbread Crust: Combine flour and sugar in medium bowl. Cut in butter until mixture resembles coarse crumbs. Press firmly in bottom and up side of 9 inch (22 cm) pie plate. Bake in 350°F (175°C) oven for about 15 minutes until golden. Let stand on wire rack to cool.

Filling: Beat first 3 ingredients in medium bowl until smooth.

Stir in next 3 ingredients.

Beat whipping cream in medium bowl until soft peaks form. Fold into cream cheese mixture. Spread evenly in crust. Freeze until set.

Topping: Beat first 3 ingredients in medium bowl until soft peaks form. Pipe or spoon over individual servings.

Arrange cherries over whipped cream. Cuts into 8 wedges.

1 wedge: 600 Calories; 42.6 g Total Fat (11.8 g Mono, 1.6 g Poly, 26.8 g Sat); 134 mg Cholesterol; 51 g Carbohydrate; 1 g Fibre; 6 g Protein; 238 mg Sodium

Pictured at right.

Lively Lime Pie

Block of cream cheese, softened	8 oz.	250 g
Can of sweetened condensed milk	11 oz.	300 mL
Lime juice	1/2 cup	125 mL
Grated lime zest (see Tip, page 56)	2 tsp.	10 mL
Graham cracker crust (9 inch, 22 cm, diameter)	1	1
Grated lime zest, for garnish		

We call it lively for a reason. This frozen lime lovely packs a wallop of tart tang. Keep in the freezer until ready to serve.

Beat cream cheese in medium bowl for about 3 minutes until smooth. Slowly add condensed milk, beating constantly until combined.

Add lime juice and lime zest. Beat well.

Spread evenly in graham crust. Freeze for about 4 hours until firm.

Garnish with lime zest. Cuts into 8 wedges.

1 wedge: 375 Calories; 20.8 g Total Fat (7.1 g Mono, 2.6 g Poly, 9.9 g Sat); 44 mg Cholesterol; 43 g Carbohydrate; 1 g Fibre; 7 g Protein; 306 mg Sodium

Pictured below.

Left: Lively Lime Pie, above
Right: Piña Colada Pie page 100

This icy strawberry treat set on top a crisp pecan crust is easy to cut, easy to eat and easy to love.

about pecans

Although the pecan may be a tough nut to crack, it's certainly not tough to love its delicious rich and buttery interior. Pecans in the shell can be stored tightly wrapped in a cool, dark place for up to six months, while pre-shelled pecans can be kept for up to three months in an airtight container in the fridge, or frozen for up to six months.

Strawberry Freeze

PECAN CRUST

Butter (or hard margarine)	3/4 cup	175 mL
All-purpose flour	1 3/4 cups	425 mL
Brown sugar, packed	1/2 cup	125 mL
Finely chopped pecans	3/4 cup	175 mL

FILLING

Egg whites (large), see Tip, page 83	2	2
Container of frozen strawberries in light syrup, partially thawed (with syrup)	15 oz.	425 g
Granulated sugar	3/4 cup	175 mL
Lemon juice	2 tbsp.	30 mL

TOPPING

Whipping cream (or 1 envelope of dessert topping, prepared)	1 cup	250 mL

Halved fresh strawberries, for garnish

Pecan Crust: Melt butter in medium saucepan on medium. Remove from heat. Add next 3 ingredients. Stir well. Spread on ungreased baking sheet with sides. Bake in 375°F (190°C) oven for 15 to 20 minutes, stirring occasionally, until browned. Remove from oven. Break up chunks. Press firmly in bottom of ungreased 10 inch (25 cm) springform pan.

Filling: Beat first 4 ingredients in large bowl on high speed for about 10 minutes until thickened and fluffy.

Topping: Beat whipping cream in small bowl until soft peaks form. Fold into strawberry mixture. Spread evenly over crust. Freeze, covered, for at least 8 hours or overnight.

Garnish with strawberries. Cuts into 16 wedges.

1 wedge: 283 Calories; 17.7 g Total Fat (6.0 g Mono, 1.7 g Poly, 9.0 g Sat); 42 mg Cholesterol; 30 g Carbohydrate; 1 g Fibre; 3 g Protein; 76 mg Sodium

Pictured on page 3 and at right.

This yummy dessert can be made several weeks ahead, but we can't guarantee that hiding it in the freezer will save it for when it's needed. It's just too irresistible! Serve with whipped cream and grated chocolate for a fancier presentation.

Frosty Peanut Butter Pie

CRUST

Butter (or hard margarine)	6 tbsp.	100 mL
Chocolate wafer crumbs	1 1/2 cups	375 mL
Icing (confectioner's) sugar	1 tbsp.	15 mL

FILLING

Vanilla ice cream, softened	1/2 cup	125 mL
Smooth peanut butter	1/3 cup	75 mL
Vanilla ice cream, softened	2 cups	500 mL
Frozen whipped topping, thawed	1 cup	250 mL
Finely chopped peanuts	3 tbsp.	50 mL

Crust: Melt butter in medium saucepan on medium. Remove from heat. Add wafer crumbs and icing sugar. Stir well. Reserve 2 tbsp. (30 mL) for topping. Press firmly in bottom and up side of 9 inch (22 cm) pie plate. Bake in 350°F (175°C) oven for 10 minutes. Cool.

Filling: Mash first amount of ice cream and peanut butter in large bowl. Gently fold in second amount of ice cream.

Fold in whipped topping and peanuts. Spread evenly in crust. Sprinkle with reserved crumb mixture. Freeze, covered, until firm. Let stand at room temperature for 10 minutes before cutting. Cuts into 8 wedges.

1 wedge: 445 Calories; 31.8 g Total Fat (6.6 g Mono, 3.2 g Poly, 16.5 g Sat); 98 mg Cholesterol; 34 g Carbohydrate; 2 g Fibre; 8 g Protein; 233 mg Sodium

Pictured at right.

Top: Mud Pie page 108
Bottom: Frosty Peanut Butter Pie, above

food fun

So whose crazy idea was it to stick something filled with ice cream into the oven? There are many theories, but the discovery that fluffy meringue could insulate a frozen centre from the oven's heat is often credited to physicist Benjamin Thompson, who studied heat resistance in the early 1800s. The resulting dish, called *omelette Norvègienne*, or Norwegian omelette, became the hottest— and coolest—dessert around!

A great, and downright healthy, treat to give the kids when they're clamouring for a sweet, cold bite to eat.

variation

Instead of using walnuts, try chopped pecans or hazelnuts.

Baked Alaska

Jam-filled jelly roll (3 – 3 1/2 inches, 7.5 – 9 cm, diameter)	1	1
Egg whites (large), room temperature	5	5
Vanilla extract	1 tsp.	5 mL
Salt	1/4 tsp.	1 mL
Granulated sugar	3/4 cup	175 mL
Vanilla ice cream	2 cups	500 mL

Cut jelly roll crosswise into eight 1/2 inch (12 mm) thick slices. Arrange slices in single layer on ungreased baking sheet.

Beat next 3 ingredients in medium bowl until soft peaks form. Add sugar, 1 tbsp. (15 mL) at a time, beating constantly until sugar is dissolved.

Place 1 scoop of ice cream in centre of each jelly roll slice. Working quickly, spread egg white mixture over ice cream scoops to edge of jelly roll slice. Freeze until set. Bake on centre rack in 450°F (230°C) oven for about 2 minutes until meringue is golden. Serve immediately. Serves 8.

1 serving: 242 Calories; 10.1 g Total Fat (0.6 g Mono, 0.1 g Poly, 5.8 g Sat); 64 mg Cholesterol; 32 g Carbohydrate; trace Fibre; 5 g Protein; 167 mg Sodium

Pictured at right.

Frozen Banana Rockets

Medium bananas	4	4
Wooden craft sticks	4	4
Vanilla yogurt	1/4 cup	60 mL
Chopped walnuts, toasted (see Tip, page 48)	1/2 cup	125 mL
Raw sunflower seeds, toasted (see Tip, page 48)	1/4 cup	60 mL

Trim 1/4 inch (6 mm) from 1 end of each banana. Insert wooden craft stick into trimmed end.

(continued on next page)

Measure yogurt into shallow dish. Spread walnuts and sunflower seeds on plate. Roll bananas in yogurt. Roll and press into walnut mixture until coated. Wrap bananas individually with plastic wrap. Freeze for about 2 hours until firm. Makes 4 rockets.

1 rocket: 272 Calories; 15.4 g Total Fat (1.4 g Mono, 7.2 g Poly, 1.7 g Sat); 1 mg Cholesterol; 32 g Carbohydrate; 5 g Fibre; 7 g Protein; 20 mg Sodium

Baked Alaska, page 106

We think whoever coined the term "Here's mud in your eye," was actually misquoted. Surely he meant "Here's to mud pie," because this rich and chocolatey pie surely deserves a toast of its own. Decorate individual servings with whipped cream, coffee beans and any extra sauce.

Mud Pie

CRUST

Butter (or hard margarine)	1/3 cup	75 mL
Chocolate wafer crumbs	1 1/2 cups	375 mL

FILLING

Coffee ice cream, softened (see Note)	6 cups	1.5 L

FUDGE SAUCE

Unsweetened chocolate baking squares (1 oz., 28 g, each), cut up	4	4
Evaporated milk	3/4 cup	175 mL
Butter (or hard margarine)	2 tbsp.	30 mL
Icing (confectioner's) sugar	2 cups	500 mL
Salt, just a pinch		
Vanilla extract	1/2 tsp.	2 mL

Crust: Melt butter in medium saucepan on medium. Remove from heat. Add wafer crumbs. Stir well. Press firmly in bottom and up side of 9 inch (22 cm) pie plate. Bake in 350°F (175°C) oven for 10 minutes. Cool.

Filling: Spread ice cream evenly in crust. Freeze until firm.

Fudge Sauce: Combine first 5 ingredients in medium saucepan. Heat and stir on medium until boiling and chocolate is melted. Reduce heat to low. Cook and stir for 5 minutes.

Add vanilla. Stir. Makes about 2 cups (500 mL) sauce. Spread 1/2 cup (125 mL) Fudge Sauce evenly over ice cream. Freeze until set. Store remaining Fudge Sauce in airtight container in refrigerator for up to 1 week or in freezer for up to 1 month. Cuts into 8 wedges.

1 wedge: 623 Calories; 40.3 g Total Fat (3.9 g Mono, 1.3 g Poly, 23.9 g Sat); 203 mg Cholesterol; 56 g Carbohydrate; 1 g Fibre; 10 g Protein; 293 mg Sodium

Pictured on page 105.

Note: If coffee ice cream isn't available, dissolve 1 tbsp. (15 mL) instant coffee granules in 2 tbsp. (30 mL) hot water. Mix into softened vanilla ice cream.

Frozen Fudge Pops

Milk	2 1/2 cups	625 mL
Granulated sugar	1/2 cup	125 mL
Box of instant chocolate pudding powder (4-serving size)	1	1

Beat all 3 ingredients on low in medium bowl until creamy and thick. Pour into freezer pop forms. Freeze for at least 8 hours or overnight. Makes about 12 fudge pops.

1 fudge pop: 87 Calories; 0.7 g Total Fat (0.3 g Mono, trace Poly, 0.4 g Sat); 3 mg Cholesterol; 19 g Carbohydrate; trace Fibre; 2 g Protein; 159 mg Sodium

Pictured on page 111.

A snap to make. And if you're looking for a treat with a little less sweetness, the sugar may be cut in half with only a touch of flavour change.

Creamy Ice Pops

Box of strawberry (or raspberry) jelly powder (gelatin)	3 oz.	85 g
Boiling water	1 cup	250 mL
Strawberry (or raspberry) yogurt	1 cup	250 mL
Cold water	1/2 cup	125 mL

Combine jelly powder and boiling water in medium heatproof bowl. Stir until jelly powder is dissolved.

Add yogurt. Stir. Add cold water. Stir. Pour into freezer pop forms. Freeze for at least 8 hours or overnight. Makes about 10 ice pops.

1 ice pop: 57 Calories; 0.3 g Total Fat (0 g Mono, 0 g Poly, 0.2 g Sat); 2 mg Cholesterol; 12 g Carbohydrate; 0 g Fibre; 2 g Protein; 51 mg Sodium

Pictured on page 111.

Make these fun and frosty treats any flavour you like by changing the varieties of yogurt and jelly powder.

tip

If you don't have freezer pop forms, use small paper cups instead. For the handle, cover the cup in tin foil, cut a small hole in the centre and insert a wooden craft stick.

A true favourite of children and adults alike. You can't go wrong with a banana split. If you'd prefer to cut the calories a tad, use light or low-fat versions of ice cream.

banana split birthday party

For your child's next birthday party, set out toppings, sauces and ice cream flavours on a table or counter, give each child a dish containing two banana halves, then let them make their own sundaes. Just make sure to set down an old tablecloth that you can easily toss in the wash, because things are bound to get sticky!

Banana Split

Large banana, halved lengthwise	1	1
Chocolate ice cream	1/4 cup	60 mL
Strawberry ice cream	1/4 cup	60 mL
Vanilla ice cream	1/4 cup	60 mL
Chocolate ice cream topping	2 tbsp.	30 mL
Strawberry jam	2 tbsp.	30 mL
Butterscotch ice cream topping	2 tbsp.	30 mL

Whipped cream, for garnish
Candied sprinkles, for garnish
Maraschino cherry, for garnish

Place banana halves on opposite sides of banana split dish. Scoop next 3 ingredients down center between banana halves.

Spoon chocolate ice cream topping over chocolate ice cream, strawberry jam over strawberry ice cream and butterscotch ice cream topping over vanilla ice cream.

Garnish with whipped cream, candied sprinkles and maraschino cherry. Serves 1.

1 serving: 846 Calories; 28.0 g Total Fat (trace Mono, 0.1 g Poly, 16.7 g Sat); 165 mg Cholesterol; 143 g Carbohydrate; 5 g Fibre; 9 g Protein; 269 mg Sodium

Pictured at right.

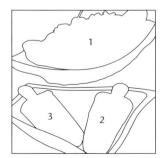

1. Banana Split, above
2. Frozen Fudge Pops, page 109
3. Creamy Ice Pops, page 109

about ice-cream makers

Ice cream makers are available in all sizes and price ranges, in styles ranging from hand-cranked to convenient self-refrigerating models. But whether high or low-tech, they all operate in the same way. A chilled outer chamber surrounds an inner chamber containing the ice cream mixture. A rotating paddle keeps the mixture moving, adding air and preventing the formation of chunky ice crystals.

White Chocolate Ice Cream

Milk	2 cups	500 mL
Granulated sugar	3/4 cup	175 mL
All-purpose flour	1 tbsp.	15 mL
Salt	1/2 tsp.	2 mL
Large egg	1	1
White chocolate baking squares (1 oz., 28 g, each), cut up	6	6
Whipping cream	2 cups	500 mL
Vanilla extract	1/2 tsp.	2 mL

Heat milk in medium heavy saucepan on medium until hot, but not boiling.

Combine next 3 ingredients in small bowl. Beat in egg until smooth. Stir into hot milk. Heat and stir for 3 minutes. Remove from heat.

Add chocolate. Stir until melted. Chill, covered, for at least 6 hours or overnight.

Stir in whipping cream and vanilla. Pour into ice-cream maker. Freeze until firm. Makes about 6 cups (1.5 L).

1/2 cup (125 mL): 280 Calories; 19.3 g Total Fat (5.7 g Mono, 0.7 g Poly, 11.8 g Sat); 72 mg Cholesterol; 24 g Carbohydrate; trace Fibre; 4 g Protein; 151 mg Sodium

Pictured at right.

Here's a refreshing, cool treat to enjoy on a warm day or following a spicy main course. Set out small dishes of chopped peanuts, sliced banana or mango and freshly chopped mint as toppings.

Vanilla Coconut Ice Cream

Cans of coconut milk (14 oz., 398 mL, each)	2	2
Milk	1 cup	250 mL
Vanilla extract	1/2 tsp.	2 mL
Egg yolks (large), see Note	10	10
Granulated sugar	1 1/2 cups	375 mL
Flaked coconut, toasted (see Tip, page 48)	1/3 cup	75 mL

Combine first 3 ingredients in large saucepan. Heat and stir on medium until hot, but not boiling. Remove from heat.

(continued on next page)

Beat egg yolks and sugar in large bowl. Slowly add hot milk mixture, stirring constantly with whisk. Return to same saucepan. Heat and stir on medium until mixture is thickened enough to coat back of metal spoon. Strain. Chill, covered, for at least 6 hours or overnight. Pour into ice-cream maker. Freeze until firm. Scoop into tall glasses or individual serving bowls.

Sprinkle with coconut. Makes about 6 cups (1.5 L).

1/2 cup (125 mL): *311 Calories; 20.6 g Total Fat (2.5 g Mono, 0.8 g Poly, 15.6 g Sat); 159 mg Cholesterol; 30 g Carbohydrate; trace Fibre; 5 g Protein; 42 mg Sodium*

Note: Egg whites can be frozen for later use.

Pictured below.

Left: White Chocolate Ice Cream, page 112
Right: Vanilla Coconut Ice Cream, page 112

This decorative dessert will leave your guests in awe of your creative talents! The richness of nuts and chocolate will satisfy any sweets lover.

Macadamia Tortoni

TORTONI

Egg white (large), room temperature (see Tip, page 83)	1	1
Whipping cream	1 cup	250 mL
Icing (confectioner's) sugar	1/3 cup	75 mL
Vanilla extract	1 tsp.	5 mL
Finely chopped macadamia nuts, toasted (see Tip, page 48)	1/3 cup	75 mL

CHOCOLATE CUPS

White candy melting wafers	3/4 cup	175 mL
Milk chocolate melting wafers	3/4 cup	175 mL

Finely chopped macadamia nuts, toasted (see Tip, page 48), for garnish
Grated chocolate, for garnish
Fresh raspberries, for garnish

Tortoni: Beat egg white in small bowl until stiff peaks form.

Using same beaters, beat next 3 ingredients in medium bowl until soft peaks form. Fold in egg white.

Fold in macadamia nuts. Spread evenly in ungreased 9 inch (22 cm) pie plate. Freeze, covered, for at least 6 hours or overnight.

Chocolate Cups: Line inside of six 6 oz. (170 mL) custard cups or small dessert dishes with foil. Heat white melting wafers in small heavy saucepan on lowest heat, stirring often, until almost melted. Do not overheat. Remove from heat. Stir until smooth. Spoon into piping bag with small round tip. Randomly pipe squiggles over sides and bottoms of foil-lined cups, using about 1 tbsp. (15 mL) for each (see photo 1). Chill for about 2 minutes until set.

Repeat with chocolate melting wafers, ensuring bottoms are coated. It's okay to have some spaces showing on sides. Chill for about 2 minutes until set. Gently peel off and discard foil (see photo 2). Makes 6 chocolate cups. Just before serving, scoop Tortoni into Chocolate Cups.

Garnish with macadamia nuts, chocolate and raspberries. Serves 6.

1 serving: 489 Calories; 35.4 g Total Fat (10.4 g Mono, 0.8 g Poly, 18.7 g Sat); 64 mg Cholesterol; 39 g Carbohydrate; 1 g Fibre; 5 g Protein; 63 mg Sodium

Pictured at right.

Strawberry Banana Frozen Yogurt

Overripe medium banana, cut into 1 inch (2.5 cm) pieces	1	1
Large fresh whole strawberries	5	5
Non-fat vanilla yogurt	1 cup	250 mL
Liquid honey	1 1/2 tsp.	7 mL
Lemon juice	1 tsp.	5 mL
Vanilla extract	1/2 tsp.	2 mL
Frozen light whipped topping, thawed	1 cup	250 mL
Halved fresh strawberries, for garnish		

Arrange banana and strawberries in single layer on baking sheet. Freeze for about 2 hours until firm.

Put next 4 ingredients and frozen fruit into food processor. Process until smooth and slushy.

Fold in whipped topping. Line 9 x 9 inch (22 x 22 cm) pan with foil, extending foil over 2 sides. Pour fruit mixture into prepared pan. Freeze for about 3 hours, stirring every 30 minutes for the first 1 1/2 hours, until firm.

Garnish individual servings with strawberries. Makes about 3 1/2 cups (875 mL).

1/2 cup (125 mL): 85 Calories; 2.4 g Total Fat (trace Mono, trace Poly, 2.3 g Sat); 1 mg Cholesterol; 14 g Carbohydrate; 1 g Fibre; 2 g Protein; 32 mg Sodium

Pictured on page 117.

Cran-Raspberry Ice

Box of raspberry jelly powder (gelatin)	3 oz.	85 g
Boiling water	1/2 cup	125 mL
Box of whole raspberries, partially thawed	10 oz.	300 g
Block of cream cheese, softened	4 oz.	125 g
Icing (confectioner's) sugar	1/4 cup	60 mL
Whole cranberry sauce	14 oz.	398 mL
Sour cream	1 cup	250 mL

(continued on next page)

Stir jelly powder into boiling water in small heatproof bowl until dissolved. Add raspberries. Stir.

Beat cream cheese and icing sugar in medium bowl until smooth. Add cranberry sauce and sour cream. Mix well. Add raspberry mixture. Stir. Pour into plastic wrap-lined loaf pan. Freeze, covered, until firm. Invert onto cutting board. Cuts into 10 slices.

1 slice: 211 Calories; 8.1 g Total Fat (2.3 g Mono, 0.3 g Poly, 5.1 g Sat); 22 mg Cholesterol; 34 g Carbohydrate; 2 g Fibre; 3 g Protein; 84 mg Sodium

Pictured below.

Left: Cran-Raspberry Ice, page 116
Right: Strawberry Banana Frozen Yogurt, page 116

about sorbet

Not all frozen desserts are created equal. Non-milk-drinkers take note: while ice cream and sherbet get their characteristic creaminess from cream and milk respectively, sorbets are decidedly lacking in the white stuff, making them lighter and more refreshing—and lower in fat—than their dairy-laden cousins. Sorbets are usually sweet, but savoury variations are also becoming quite popular as palate cleansers between dinner courses.

Ginger Sorbet With Grilled Mangoes

GINGER SORBET		
Water	2 cups	500 mL
Granulated sugar	1 1/2 cups	375 mL
Finely grated gingerroot	1 tbsp.	15 mL
Egg white (large), see Tip, page 83	1	1
GRILLED MANGOES		
Medium mangoes	3	3
Butter (or hard margarine), melted	2 tbsp.	30 mL
Brown sugar, packed	1/2 tbsp.	7 mL
Ground cinnamon	1/2 tsp.	2 mL

Ginger Sorbet: Combine water and sugar in large saucepan. Heat and stir on low until sugar is dissolved. Bring to a boil. Remove from heat. Add ginger. Pour into 9 x 9 inch (22 x 22 cm) pan. Freeze for about 3 hours until set.

Spoon into food processor. Add egg white. Process until smooth. Makes about 3 cups (750 mL) sorbet. Return to same pan. Freeze until set.

Grilled Mangoes: Preheat gas barbecue to medium. Slice through flat side of 1 mango near centre, carving around curve of pit. Repeat down other side. Using small sharp knife, score flesh in small diamonds until tip of knife hits skin but does not go through. Repeat with remaining mangoes.

Combine remaining 3 ingredients in small bowl. Brush mango flesh with butter mixture. Cook mango, skin-side up, on ungreased grill for 6 to 8 minutes until soft and lightly browned. Transfer to plate. Brush mango flesh with remaining butter mixture. Using hands, press on skin side with thumbs, turning each section inside out and spreading diamonds apart. Serve with Ginger Sorbet. Serves 6.

1 serving: 246 Calories; 3.9 g Total Fat (1 g Mono, 0.2 g Poly, 2.4 g Sat); 10 mg Cholesterol; 54 g Carbohydrate; 2 g Fibre; 1 g Protein; 39 mg Sodium

Pictured at right.

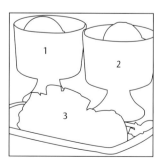

1. Raspberry Freeze, page 121
2. Kiwifruit Sorbet, page 120
3. Ginger Sorbet With Grilled Mangoes, above

Mango Melon Sorbet

Cubed cantaloupe	2 cups	500 mL
Large mango, cubed	1	1
Granulated sugar	1/4 cup	60 mL
Lime juice	1/4 cup	60 mL

Spread cantaloupe in single layer on baking sheet. Freeze for about 1 1/2 hours until firm. Transfer to blender or food processor.

Add remaining 3 ingredients. Process until smooth. Spread evenly in ungreased 1 1/2 quart (1.5 L) shallow baking dish. Freeze, covered, for about 2 hours until almost firm. Scrape and stir to break up ice crystals. Freeze until firm. Let stand in refrigerator for 1 hour before serving. Makes about 3 cups (750 mL).

1/2 cup (125 mL): 58 Calories; 0.2 g Total Fat (trace Mono, 0.1 g Poly, trace Sat); 0 mg Cholesterol; 15 g Carbohydrate; 1 g Fibre; 1 g Protein; 9 mg Sodium

Kiwifruit Sorbet

Granulated sugar	2/3 cup	150 mL
Water	2/3 cup	150 mL
Ripe kiwifruit, coarsely chopped	8	8
Lemon juice	2 tbsp.	30 mL
Sliced ripe kiwifruit, for garnish		

Combine sugar and water in small saucepan. Heat and stir on low until sugar is dissolved. Bring to a boil. Do not stir. Remove from heat. Cool completely.

Put kiwifruit, lemon juice and sugar mixture into food processor. Process until smooth. Pour into plastic wrap-lined 9 x 9 inch (22 x 22 cm) pan. Freeze for 2 hours. Remove from pan. Discard plastic wrap. Cut fruit mixture into pieces. Transfer to food processor. Process until smooth. Return to same pan, lined with plastic wrap. Freeze for 4 to 6 hours until firm. Let stand at room temperature for 5 minutes before serving.

Garnish individual servings with kiwifruit. Makes about 3 1/3 cups (825 mL).

1/2 cup (125 mL): 125 Calories; 0.5 g Total Fat (trace Mono, 0.3 g Poly, trace Sat); 0 mg Cholesterol; 31 g Carbohydrate; 3 g Fibre; 1 g Protein; 2.8 mg Sodium

Pictured on page 119.

Raspberry Freeze

A chilly treat that will melt the heart of the most fussy eater. This Freeze is yummy, light and refreshing.

Homogenized (or 2%) milk	2 1/2 cups	625 mL
Granulated sugar	1 cup	250 mL
Salt, sprinkle		
Envelope of unflavoured gelatin (about 1 tbsp., 15 mL)	1/4 oz.	7 g
Container of frozen raspberries in syrup, thawed	15 oz.	425 g
Lemon juice	1 tbsp.	15 mL
Egg whites (large), room temperature (see Tip, page 83)	2	2
Fresh raspberries (optional)	3/4 cup	175 mL

Combine first 3 ingredients in medium saucepan. Sprinkle gelatin over milk mixture. Let stand for 1 minute. Heat and stir on low until gelatin and sugar are dissolved. Remove from heat. Cool.

Put raspberries with syrup and lemon juice into blender. Process until smooth. Strain through sieve into small bowl. Discard seeds. Stir into cooled milk mixture. Pour into 9 × 13 inch (22 × 33 cm) pan. Freeze for about 2 hours, stirring occasionally, until slushy. Scrape into large bowl. Beat on high until foamy.

Using clean beaters, beat egg whites in small bowl until soft peaks form. Fold into raspberry mixture. Return to same pan. Freeze for at least 8 hours or overnight.

Serve with raspberries. Makes about 6 cups (1.5 L).

1/2 cup (125 mL): 156 Calories; 1.7 g Total Fat (0.5 g Mono, 0.1 g Poly, 1.0 g Sat); 7 mg Cholesterol; 34 g Carbohydrate; 1 g Fibre; 3 g Protein; 45 mg Sodium

Pictured on page 119.

Daydream of being in a café in Florence while you enjoy our peachy keen gelato. Serve right out of the freezer because the orange bowls will only keep their shape for about 15 minutes.

Peach Gelato

Half-and-half cream	1 1/4 cups	300 mL
Granulated sugar	1/3 cup	75 mL
Salt	1/8 tsp.	0.5 mL
Unflavoured gelatin (about half 1/4 oz., 7 g, envelope)	1 1/2 tsp.	7 mL
Can of sliced peaches, drained	14 oz.	398 mL
Peach schnapps (or peach brandy), optional	2 tbsp.	30 mL
Egg white (large), room temperature (see Tip, page 83)	1	1
ORANGE BLOSSOM BOWLS (optional)		
Granulated sugar	1/2 cup	125 mL
Water	1/2 cup	125 mL
Medium navel oranges	5 – 6	5 – 6

Fresh mint leaves, for garnish

Combine first 3 ingredients in medium saucepan. Sprinkle gelatin over top. Let stand for 1 minute. Heat and stir on low until gelatin and sugar are dissolved. Remove from heat. Cool.

Put peaches into blender or food processor. Process until smooth. Add to gelatin mixture. Add schnapps. Stir.

Beat egg white in medium bowl until soft peaks form. Fold peach mixture into egg white. Pour into ungreased 9 x 9 inch (22 x 22 cm) pan. Freeze, uncovered, for about 1 hour until slushy. Transfer to separate medium bowl. Beat on high for about 2 minutes until foamy and light. Spread evenly in same pan. Freeze, covered, for at least 8 hours or overnight. Makes about 2 1/2 cups (625 mL) gelato.

Orange Blossom Bowls: Combine sugar and water in small saucepan. Bring to a boil. Reduce heat to medium-low. Simmer, uncovered, for 5 minutes, stirring occasionally. Cool slightly. Chill until cold.

(continued on next page)

Cut oranges crosswise into 1/16 inch (1.5 mm) slices with very sharp knife or slicer. Slices must be very thin to form bowl shape. Discard ends. Line 10 small dessert bowls with plastic wrap. Dip slices, 1 at a time, into sugar syrup. Arrange, slightly overlapping, around sides of prepared dessert dishes. Lay 1 orange slice flat on bottom of each bowl (see Note). Cover with plastic wrap, pressing down against orange slices. Freeze for at least 6 hours or overnight. Unwrap and remove bowls. Peel off and discard plastic wrap. Keep bowls frozen until ready to serve. Makes 10 bowls. Just before serving, scoop small balls of Peach Gelato into frozen orange bowls.

Garnish with mint leaves. Serves 10.

1 serving (without bowl): 100 Calories; 3.7 g Total Fat (1.1 g Mono, 0.1 g Poly, 2.2 g Sat); 12 mg Cholesterol; 16 g Carbohydrate; 1 g Fibre; 1 g Protein; 51 mg Sodium

Pictured below.

Note: There may be some sugar syrup and orange slices left over. Use in punch or other beverage or serve with ice cream.

Throughout this book measurements are given in Conventional and Metric measure. To compensate for differences between the two measurements due to rounding, a full metric measure is not always used. The cup used is the standard 8 fluid ounce. Temperature is given in degrees Fahrenheit and Celsius. Baking pan measurements are in inches and centimetres as well as quarts and litres. An exact metric conversion is given on this page as well as the working equivalent (Metric Standard Measure).

Pans

Conventional – Inches	Metric – Centimetres
8 × 8 inch	20 × 20 cm
9 × 9 inch	22 × 22 cm
9 × 13 inch	22 × 33 cm
10 × 15 inch	25 × 38 cm
11 × 17 inch	28 × 43 cm
8 × 2 inch round	20 × 5 cm
9 × 2 inch round	22 × 5 cm
10 × 4 1/2 inch tube	25 × 11 cm
8 × 4 × 3 inch loaf	20 × 10 × 7.5 cm
9 × 5 × 3 inch loaf	22 × 12.5 × 7.5 cm

Oven Temperatures

Fahrenheit (°F)	Celsius (°C)	Fahrenheit (°F)	Celsius (°C)
175°	80°	350°	175°
200°	95°	375°	190°
225°	110°	400°	205°
250°	120°	425°	220°
275°	140°	450°	230°
300°	150°	475°	240°
325°	160°	500°	260°

Spoons

Conventional Measure	Metric Exact Conversion Millilitre (mL)	Metric Standard Measure Millilitre (mL)
1/8 teaspoon (tsp.)	0.6 mL	0.5 mL
1/4 teaspoon (tsp.)	1.2 mL	1 mL
1/2 teaspoon (tsp.)	2.4 mL	2 mL
1 teaspoon (tsp.)	4.7 mL	5 mL
2 teaspoons (tsp.)	9.4 mL	10 mL
1 tablespoon (tbsp.)	14.2 mL	15 mL

Cups

1/4 cup (4 tbsp.)	56.8 mL	60 mL
1/3 cup (5 1/3 tbsp.)	75.6 mL	75 mL
1/2 cup (8 tbsp.)	113.7 mL	125 mL
2/3 cup (10 2/3 tbsp.)	151.2 mL	150 mL
3/4 cup (12 tbsp.)	170.5 mL	175 mL
1 cup (16 tbsp.)	227.3 mL	250 mL
4 1/2 cups	1022.9 mL	1000 mL (1 L)

Dry Measurements

Conventional Measure Ounces (oz.)	Metric Exact Conversion Grams (g)	Metric Standard Measure Grams (g)
1 oz.	28.3 g	28 g
2 oz.	56.7 g	57 g
3 oz.	85.0 g	85 g
4 oz.	113.4 g	125 g
5 oz.	141.7 g	140 g
6 oz.	170.1 g	170 g
7 oz.	198.4 g	200 g
8 oz.	226.8 g	250 g
16 oz.	453.6 g	500 g
32 oz.	907.2 g	1000 g (1 kg)

Casseroles

Canada & Britain		United States	
Standard Size Casserole	Exact Metric Measure	Standard Size Casserole	Exact Metric Measure
1 qt. (5 cups)	1.13 L	1 qt. (4 cups)	900 mL
1 1/2 qts. (7 1/2 cups)	1.69 L	1 1/2 qts. (6 cups)	1.35 L
2 qts. (10 cups)	2.25 L	2 qts. (8 cups)	1.8 L
2 1/2 qts. (12 1/2 cups)	2.81 L	2 1/2 qts. (10 cups)	2.25 L
3 qts. (15 cups)	3.38 L	3 qts. (12 cups)	2.7 L
4 qts. (20 cups)	4.5 L	4 qts. (16 cups)	3.6 L
5 qts. (25 cups)	5.63 L	5 qts. (20 cups)	4.5 L

Tip Index

Recipe Index